ANGELS
at Work

God's Providence... An Autobiography

JOHN G. (JACK) GREEN

WESTBOW
PRESS®
A DIVISION OF THOMAS NELSON
& ZONDERVAN

WestBow Press books may be ordered through booksellers or by contacting:

WestBow Press
A Division of Thomas Nelson & Zondervan
1663 Liberty Drive
Bloomington, IN 47403
www.westbowpress.com
1 (866) 928-1240

Scripture quotations taken from The Holy Bible, New International Version® NIV® Copyright © 1973 1978 1984 2011 by Biblica, Inc. TM. Used by permission. All rights reserved worldwide.

ISBN: 978-1-9736-8641-5 (sc)
ISBN: 978-1-9736-8643-9 (hc)
ISBN: 978-1-9736-8642-2 (e)

Library of Congress Control Number: 2020903120

Print information available on the last page.

WestBow Press rev. date: 02/26/2020

Contents

INTRODUCTION

Show me your ways, Lord, teach me your paths. (Psalm 25:4)

For those who have faith that God's providential care is designed to help believers follow the plan He has for a life of service, here is our heavenly Father's promise: "For I know the plans I have for you, declares the Lord, plans to prosper you and not to harm you, plans to give you hope and a future" (Jeremiah 29:11).

"God has the sovereign ability to fashion everything according to His purposes and His plans that He has for our lives. And for that, I am eternally grateful" (Kathy Barnette, Decision, September 2019).

The basic premise of this book has to do with God's plan for individual life. Here is a basic understanding of how the Bible reveals God's plan for humanity. The eternal plan of God for all believers is that they share their faith experience in the belief that Jesus Christ is the Savior of a sinful and dying world. In doing this, believers become servants of God. Some do it as the primary work of their lives, and all true believers do it in daily life whatever their pursuits.

The providence of God is the care He provides daily as His plan is being followed. Eternal providence assures believers that the resurrection of Jesus Christ will be experienced by all souls in completion of their salvation.

The Holy Spirit and entities known as angels of God provide personal guidance and care as God's eternal plan for an individual is followed. When following the plan of God, an individual will know His providential care by hindsight.

This book is a catalog of events known only by a look back. It is the life of two who lived with personal faith, a day-by-day walk as God led them. Actions and their consequences are not based on common sense, which can be the enemy of faith. Nor is it understood by rational thought. It is a work only a living God can perform.

God's plan for believers requires active faith. It does not assume believers can do whatever they please believing God will intervene for safety or life. No, it is the opposite. By faith in a living God who loves, cares, and delivers His servants while following His will, He provides believers with His Spirit, the Holy Spirit. Therefore, when Jesus Christ is Lord, He guides, and as believers, we follow.

It must be made clear—we do not rejoice in the plan and providence of God with an idea of sitting down and expecting God to act. No; it is the plan that glorifies God made possible by His providential care in daily life. It is supremely a life of faith in the Lord God almighty made possible by the blood sacrifice of Jesus Christ.

This personal accounting of events is my effort to share the care and guidance given to obedient servants who live lives of faith in God. While the following events and thoughts center on the lives of two Christians, it is not about them but about Him and what He has done for and through them. It could be told by millions of faithful servants of our God.

There are two groups of people recognized here, the unredeemed and the redeemed. While this is not a course in theology, we believe every soul will be accountable to our God, who created them. They will experience a destiny God has given them permission to choose for themselves.

Every soul born of God is given the power and grace to choose to be unredeemed or redeemed before death. We know it as humankind's free will. The unredeemed are those who have not accepted forgiveness under the shed and saving blood of Jesus Christ. Their plan is not of God but of themselves. This is best explained when we see how the unredeemed create circumstances that affect their lives and cause them to suffer the consequences.

God does not remove freedom from His children to make wrong or evil choices when He grants forgiveness. In a world turned evil, believers learn to get continuous and daily forgiveness for sin. It is submission to the plan of the One who calls, and it is the same for every believer whose Lord is Jesus Christ.

Recorded here is the life and ministerial history of two redeemed under the forgiving blood of the Lord Jesus Christ. It reveals how the Holy Spirit prepares and guides God's redeemed. Unexplainable activities are attributed to the love and power of God.

The Spirit's influence brought a desire for my wife and I to follow God's plan. It was our choice for life. Therefore, references and events recorded here reflect our obedience in following Him in yielding prayer with leadership by God's Spirit.

When I record here that God spoke in certain terms about a ministry or service move, this may be of concern to some. Here is a warning. This is the holy ground, which is difficult to plow. It does not come with the same "light from heaven" in a single moment like that of the apostle Paul (Acts 9:1–19).

The voice of God is extremely personal. When two are working together in God's kingdom, one may hear what is determined to be God's direction for an event or for life. It is then that the Holy Spirit gives leadership in oneness to His servants made possible by two who yield to One voice.

Godly servants, especially those in daily ministry, are bathed in the attitude and act of prayer. At any time when in worship, personal prayer, quiet times, or in the throes of a personal decision, the Holy Spirit may speak to God's servants. He is available for any servant who desires to know His will. His leading is a response to personal faith at a time when God has a message about a problem, need, or life work.

Total surrender to the leadership of the Holy Spirit is basic. When there is no obedience to God through prayer, there are negative consequences for the believer. For those whose lives are devoted to lifetime work for God, disobedience harms kingdom work as it is not the will of God but the will of humanity.

All believers have the glorious privilege of having a conversation with the creating Lord of the universe. Prayer is a learned experience that is deepened with time in a maturing believer. It begins with repentance at salvation. As a never-ending growth factor, personal prayer provides the joy and hope of a believer. The Holy Spirit joins the faithful interceding for the concerns of the believer (Romans 8:26–27). Daily repentance respects God's rejection of all sin in His presence. Our world is under the influence of the Evil One. No one is exempt from temptation. Protection from that influence and guidance is available only by personal choice. The heavenly Father is the only power available to believers to help them deal with evil. Satan is defeated only by the power of God. In Jesus's prayer prior to the crucifixion, He asked on our behalf, "Father, protect them from the evil one" (John 17:15).

The Bible is the written authority of God for believers. Holy means separate, unlike any other. Nothing in human history has ever been written that exceeds the complete revealing, the revelation, of the loving God who created humanity to live with Him for eternity.

The following is the personal record of God's providence, His plan, for two redeemed sinners. It covers more than seventy years. It is a record of joy, need, and failure under an eternal promise of love, care, forgiveness, and usefulness by a watchful heavenly Father.

Implementation of God's plan has two dimensions or elements. Our Father does not do all the work! His plan is for believers to put faithful effort into whatever they are called to do. When the servant has done all that is possible in whatever circumstances prevailing, our Father will dispatch an entity human or otherwise to complete the assigned task! In God's Holy Word, they are called angels.

While we served in six churches and in South Korea, fellow Christians were with us as brothers and sisters. Some were more obedient to the Father than either of us were, but this is not about them.

One of the two servants, Mary Edna, my soulmate for seventy-two years, has gone to be with the Lord. Her faithfulness exceeded mine.

Her love for me and our family is still active. It was of God. She had a quiet, attractive faith that led souls to Jesus Christ and built lifetime relationships. I find consolation in knowing she has eternal joy in the presence of our Lord.

Our story is recorded as if both of us were sitting with you in a personal conversation telling of God's love and plan as it was experienced by two ordinary believers in the redeeming grace of our heavenly Father.

The life story prior to ministry is a look back at how God's angels fashioned two lives in preparation for kingdom service. The events chronicled compose the story of how God implements his plan with providential care.

This story follows God's preparation in our childhood and early adulthood. The work of God through two of His children follows with one major interlude, which is recorded.

My life began with a miraculous birth experience. Elementary and high school led to marriage to a beautiful, young, believing woman who came from a godly family. I had two periods of active military duty. Intermingled with these events, God opened the door for the glory years of serving as pastor of five stateside churches and twelve years serving as pastoral missionaries in South Korea.

In my recording of my life events, I want no one to be under the influence of fantasy. My wife and I faced times of turmoil, doubt, and difficulty. God's call does not make one into some figure of a life Disney would film. No one believes service in the Lord's ministry is a cakewalk. This is why His providence and care were always needed; His plan had the preeminence. His basic requirement was faith!

We will glorify the wonderful providence of God, which any soul who serves the Lord can expect and trust. The use of angelic activity was clear; it left an indelible memory of God's grace and love.

The events and activities here were as real as life. Every recorded act is related as clearly as memory and records provided.

In controlling events and circumstances of daily activities of a believer, God exercises benevolent, loving care. There are no accidents or circumstances beyond His control; that was confirmed to us daily. Much of it is recorded here.

Circumstances are always under divine control. A great example is when God told Abraham that Sarah was to have a son. Sarah laughed. Abraham had lived a century. When Sarah gave birth to Isaac, his family became the ethnic group out of which came our Savior (Genesis 18).

Studying and experiencing the simplicity of God's movements in singular events may bring one to worship and adoration. God's providential care in ordinary events stirs the heart and inspires greater faith in souls who seek Him.

A society with television, internet, and publicly accepted and approved ungodly activity presents problems. There has been a slow but obvious removal of worship or mention of God in our national life. His presence in the daily decisions of those elected to govern and lead is being slowly removed.

At one time, atheists hesitated to be publicly identified, but in this hour, they are boastful and not hesitant to take believers to courts of law to remove evidence or practices of their faith.

With these influences, the life God intended has little meaning for multitudes. This contrasts with the power of the Almighty revealed by His love, grace, and mercy to those who serve Him.

Experiencing God's providential care is convincing of His plan and care. With every recall, looking back as to God's care, there was more adoration, a deepening of resolve that resulted in the greater assurance of God's presence and protection.

No soul is a robot. God's basic requirement in controlling daily activities is the believing faith explained earlier. This must be joined with yielding obedience by a surrendered child of God.

Providential care of God is active for every believer. Those called into vocational ministry are prone to recognize it more quickly than most Christians. Remaining alive may depend upon it. No assurance spiritual or otherwise cancels the human instinct for survival. Human impulse avoids death, yet it is a reality. No one can avoid it.

For believers, when Jesus is Lord, death "has no sting." In the same message of this promise, Paul told Christians that death brought victory! (1 Corinthians 15).

Our testimony is to the fact of assurance. God did not give us a safety net to escape from death. It was a path to live; a door was opened for us to share the good news of Jesus Christ with a dying world. Each day was the opportunity to lead others to a saving knowledge of Jesus Christ. As God's plan unfolded, we faced wonderful challenges without fear. Being held in the hand of God in His service brought us glory that made life glorious and death a precious event for eternity with God.

Serving God as a lifetime commitment can be tiring and trying. When daily prayer is followed by reading and studying scripture, God gives needed strength and enlightenment, the answer to humanity's drain. Service becomes a means to experience the glory and wonder of life. For every valley, there is a mountaintop. The reverse is also true. We were sometimes tired but never bored.

The need to maintain an attitude of repentance is a basic requirement. When redeemed sinners ask for and receive daily forgiveness, God's power becomes available. There is an awareness that the hand of God is providing His guidance with total security. For active servants, there are moments of caution but no doubt; there are moments of peril but no doubt. God is in control!

This telling of God's work is a tribute to Him and His glory. He has made it possible for me to tell of His wonderful guiding and leading by the quiet but sure voice of His Spirit.

CHAPTER 1

The Basis of Service

Flesh gives birth to flesh but the Spirit gives birth to spirit. (John 3:6)

Belief in Jesus Christ has certain requirements. It begins with repentance from sin, which brings God's forgiveness. The result is a yielding to Him as Lord of life forever. The Bible is the book of instruction, guidance, and revelation for all God desires from believers.

Whether it is God's call to service in a local church or to a lifetime of vocational ministry, there is a single biblical verse that describes it: "For me to live is Christ and to die is gain" (Philippians 1:21).

This lifestyle is a mystery to the non-Christian. Here it is made clear: "God has chosen to make known among the Gentiles the glorious riches of this mystery, which is Christ in you, the hope of glory" (Colossians 1:27).

When believers display a different lifestyle that glorifies our Lord, they become examples of what can be accomplished by the power of God. Jesus tells us how to live that glorious life in the Gospels. The apostle Paul made it plain how God would lead the lives of the called servants who had received His hope in their hearts: "I have been crucified with Christ and I no longer live, but Christ lives in me. The life I now live in the body, I live by faith in the Son of God, who loved me and gave himself for me" (Galatians 2:20).

Gave is a verb in the past tense; for us, it meant, "Jesus keeps on giving." The Bible says believers are saints. Believers are not free from sin, but they are forgiven of sin as believers and followers.

Personal conduct is decided daily. These verses speak to God's activity in Jesus Christ that enables the call to live for Him free of sin in His total forgiveness.

When one is free from past sin through repentance and faith in Jesus Christ, God's forgiveness results in a new heart and mind. It is a walk from darkness into Light. This can be called plan A, God's plan.

Providential guidance and care are the results of salvation. They are available for the unsaved in any land at any time when believers yield to Jesus Christ in repentance and forgiveness and make Him the Lord of their lives.

Without the redeeming and enlightening power of Jesus, Christ life is under plan B, a totally human plan. Those who deny the Lord suffer circumstances reflecting that choice. Sadly, we are living in a world of plan B souls. These souls are on the hearts and minds of believers. God commands the saved to share His love with the unsaved (Matthew 28:19).

The desire to rescue fellow humans is basic in the Christian call of God for salvation. While this is the purpose for every redeemed soul, God calls some to make this a life purpose. This is the basis for a surrender to the call of God for vocational service in the kingdom. Meeting this specific human need becomes a full-time activity, a new course of life for a believer. This was our call.

The new life in Jesus Christ is more than what most people know as light; it is a heavenly floodlight made possible by the Holy Spirit. The first desire a yielding spirit experiences with this Light is to have it the rest of life on earth. It comes with the promise of being in it for eternity. It is a hallelujah time!

This Light, the presence and daily guidance of Jesus's Spirit in the believer, can be experienced for life. The Spirit of God makes repentance of sin possible. His presence with total forgiveness of sin brings eternal Light. It is the basis for those who yield their lives for service in the kingdom of God as a primary vocation.

An awareness of the importance of God's gift of His Spirit is primary. God's Word makes it plain.

> These are the things God has revealed to us by his Spirit. The Spirit searches all things, even the deep things of God. For who knows a person's thoughts except for their own spirit within them?
>
> In the same way, no one knows the thoughts of God except the Spirit of God. What we have received is not the spirit of the world, but the Spirit who is from God, so that we may understand what God has freely given us. This is what we speak, not in words taught us by human wisdom but in words taught by the Spirit, explaining spiritual realities with Spirit-taught words.
>
> The person without the Spirit does not accept the things that come from the Spirit of God but considers them foolishness and cannot understand them because they are discerned only through the Spirit.
>
> The person with the Spirit makes judgments about all things, but such a person is not subject to merely human judgments: "Who has known the mind of the Lord to instruct him?" But we have the mind of Christ. (1 Corinthians 2:10–15)

The power switch in the human heart that leads to repentance is a dimmer switch that can dim the Light. A believer is privileged with free will, God's gift to every soul He creates. This freedom was the reason Adam and Eve could choose to sin in the Garden of Eden.

In daily service, it is not rare to meet those who apparently yielded in true repentance to Christ but have grown cold. For them, satisfying self was more important than life in Jesus Christ was. Some lean heavily on God's promise of eternal life but disregard God's commands for a continual relationship with Him and daily service to Him. As to nonbelievers, the world is full of Satan's servants dangling their lifestyles before God's children. They are tremendously successful judging by what we can see in our world in actions as well as in media of all types. It is quite easy for the children of God's creation to be comfortable in our world and live as if there were no God.

In contrast, some of the children of God in redemption find it difficult to live as God commands. While a redeemed life is very rewarding, it is not an easy life in today's world.

Facing an unbelieving world daily, believers may reach the moment when faith is present but exhausted or frightened by unfriendly activity. If faith is maintained, God's providential care becomes active and evident in these and all circumstances. God acts in response to the servant staying the course by faith. His plan for a believer is the key to and the basis of all that follows.

A kingdom worker knows the basics of faithfulness. It is the result of Bible study with worship at home and in church. This is paired with an active life of prayer—conversation with God about daily praise, forgiveness, intercessions, needs, and wants led by His Spirit.

True believers and Bible students know the promises from God concerning the here and the hereafter. As spiritual and physical maturing occurs, there is greater awareness regarding faith in a living God. This is difficult for many and especially the young as it threatens their social lives, which in our world have become extremely hedonistic—all about self-worship.

Society makes unredeemed lives comfortable. The disintegration of the family structure is increasing. Normal social conversations give way to eyes focused on smartphones. In this social atmosphere, the last thing most want to hear is someone speaking about God's providence and love for believers.

Jesus Christ, the complete revelation of God, was seen by relatively few people when He walked the earth. Faith in Him makes His life, death, burial, and resurrection as real as daylight for repentant, obedient Christians. When one experiences a walk with Jesus, one has something to share.

A holy God does not permit sin to come into His presence. He provided a way out. It is the reason for the crucifixion of Jesus Christ. Every soul created by God can know His love. Jesus's death and resurrection provided believers the way to know God's love, grace, mercy, and forgiveness. This fulfills the plan God has for each soul on earth.

There are everyday matters no one can explain including the creation and birth of a baby. Science tells of the physical while God reveals the spiritual. We know every child is the work of a loving God who is in ultimate control of the events of our lives whether that is acknowledged or not.

Every act in human life produces its consequences. God permits it. The evidence of our freedom is the privilege to make choices. Humanity either suffers or profits from the results of choice.

Non-Christians have only human resources to deal with the negatives produced by their decisions. The redeemed have the guiding hand of God. The psalmist wrote of the life of obedient believers: "The Lord will watch over your coming and going now and forevermore" (Psalm 121:8). Glory! This is the basis for our service.

CHAPTER 2

Providence, Angels, and Obedience

What is impossible with man is possible with God.
(Luke 18:22)

C hristian service for those who are faithful is a glorious, joy-filled life and journey on the way to glory. This was our experience that led to our desire to share it.

While we enjoyed the glory of God over and around His servants, the following is how we have seen this world from the viewpoint of God's servants. For the unfaithful, it is a riddle wrapped in a lifelong paradox of the seen and unseen; it left multiple questions about life here and in the hereafter unanswered.

The assessment that follows about our world does not take away the dignity of humankind placed in us by our Creator. The observation of the world condition is not made with a cold heart but with a heart that is breaking for those who need to know our Lord Christ.

As former missionaries, our journey has provided truth about all citizens of our world. Humanity will invent a god if the true God is not revealed or taught to them. The hallmark of Christianity is social grace with heavenly love and forgiveness.

Without a living God, the world has a single goal—survival. Like animal survival, it is for the superiority and control of others. The result is the destruction of life. This is how our world operates.

The possibility of a higher sphere and purpose of life is the work of a loving God who created humankind. His desire is eternal fellowship with His created ones.

The public life of many does not reflect their need for a faith that glorifies God and stabilizes life. We have developed a social atmosphere in which humanity gears itself toward wealth, popularity, and self-satisfaction. When difficulties come with a threat to wealth, position, or life, those in high standing often appear as persons who need our prayers.

Dependence upon self, humanity's gratitude, and social success is a poor substitute for dependence on God, who loves, forgives, and redeems while raising believers to a standard higher than what society applauds. It is a lifestyle that proves God made all humanity equal. The most important relationship in our world was made possible when Jesus said, "I am the way, the truth, and the life" (John 14:6).

Now and historically, true believers have become targets; they suffer punishment or death for believing and serving a living God. In recent history, citizens of an Eastern country were asked to tell the questioners if they were Christians. Fifty who stood for Christ were pushed into an open ditch and received bullets in their heads.

There will always be martyrs for Christ. In many countries, it is by the providence of God that believers survive. Faith in a resurrected Lord is the key. This sustains one in situations in which God permits pain. God uses events in the lives of the faithful to strengthen their faith. The biblical Job proves this.

God protects His trusting servants. The apostle Paul describes how God provides despite suffering and pain: "We are hard-pressed on every side, but not crushed; perplexed, but not in despair; persecuted but not abandoned; struck down, but not destroyed" (1 Corinthians 4:8–9).

Psalm 115 contains a comparison between the God of believers and idols built by humankind. A man-made idol, which is nothing more than a piece of human property, cannot address the needs of those who worship it.

Evidence of the providence of God seems to be on every page of God's Bible. We read how God is personally involved in the life of the faithful. A good example and clear evidence of this are in the survival of the Israelites in peril. A perfect example is in 2 Chronicles 14–15. Asa, the king of Judah, knew years of peace. He was told, "The Lord is with you when you are with him. If you seek him, he will be found by you, but if you forsake him, he will forsake you." Asa believed the prophet and was obedient to God.

When the neighboring Cushites rose to destroy Judah, we read the following: "Then Asa called to the Lord his God and said, 'Lord there is no one like you to help the powerless against the mighty. Help us, Lord, our God, for we rely on you and your name.'"

God's answer reveals His providential care over believers. "The Lord struck down the Cushite before Asa and Judah." How? It is not recorded, but believers know it was the work and care of God that empowered a small country to win a big victory.

Such records are numerous; they put a spotlight on God's providence. This provides success for those who God knows are in the minority, those who are in peril, those who have no answer for a problem or survival when doing God's work as His servants.

God's providence is not just for the favored few. It is available for the scholar and the uneducated, the skilled and unskilled regardless of color, gender, or nationality.

There is no rational explanation for God's providence, but it is evident when faithful servants have His deliverance when everything seems to have gone against them. It is one of His unexplainable attributes that reveal His love, grace, mercy, and forgiveness for His obedient children. We have always heard, "God will take care of you." Yes, He will, but it is a result of faith in His providential care.

We can experience but not understand God's providence. All obedient Christians experience His providence. This does not remove them from occasional fear of circumstances, but it provides them satisfaction. In life or death, we are assured God provides! There is always caution. Someone wrote, "When it is a question of the providential will of God, wait for God to act."

Here, we are discussing happenings that do not fit the pattern of normal human activity; they are the work of a loving Father. Faith in Him is the basis for a relationship in His care. Believers reveal their faith and life in God's Son, Jesus Christ, by their actions and perseverance.

While we expect God's care when we answer His call, the promise of His providential care removes fear of the present and future. The called have the assurance that the God they serve will give them His care. It is reserved for those who believe in the blood sacrifice of the Lord Jesus Christ and trust Him in obedience for a new life here and hereafter (John 3:16).

Many believe they are exempt from trouble when they become Christians. Here is Jesus Christ's explanation: "I have told you these things, so that in me you may have peace. In this world, you will have trouble. But take heart! I have overcome the world" (John 16:33).

It is our prayer in sharing that the reader will experience the joy and thrill that came to us in our spiritual adventure of faith. We attribute every work to God's glory!

This is not a theology of angels. The use of angels as a part of God's providential care is not left to substantive guessing; it is clear to believers based on actual events. God's angels participate in carrying out His plan for the faithful. Our Bible is replete with examples of angelic participation in the lives of believers and nonbelievers.

Angels come in many forms—celestial, human, and whatever God chooses for the moment or event. Those following God's plan and experiencing His providence may or may not know the angels God uses for His providential care.

On one occasion, God used an animal to reveal His word to Balaam, one of his followers (Numbers 22:21ff). While this may seem strange, it is an extreme example of how God's plan for believers is revealed or implemented. It is the providence of God—what He does for His believing children.

Look closely at the birth of two important persons when studying angelic participation in human life. In the birth records of John the Baptist and Jesus, the gospels tell us God used angels to inform their parents of the names designated for them and the providential purpose for their lives.

There has been an evolution in the use of celestial angels who were primarily informative servants of God as revealed in our Bible. The record reveals that angels were primarily used to guide God's prophets and participating believers in recorded activities prior to and after the birth, life, death, and resurrection of Jesus Christ.

In the book of Acts, angelic care of those forming the basis for Christ's church, the kingdom of God on earth, was apparent to those involved; they were constantly aware of God's providence through angelic appearances and guidance. These were times when the Spirit of God revealed His purpose or guidance to them.

Presently, Jesus is the voice and direction of God for every ordinary and critical moment of a believer's life. The Holy Spirit, Jesus's Spirit, is in the heart of every true believer for information, guidance, and assurance of God's care and love.

Here is the promise given to His faithful followers.

> If you love me, keep my commands. And I will ask the Father, and he will give you another advocate to help you and be with you forever ... the Spirit of truth. The world cannot accept him nor know him. But you know him, for he lives with you and will be in you. I will not leave you as orphans; I will come to you. Before long, the world will not see me anymore, but you will see me. On that day you will realize that I am in my Father, and you are in me, and I am in you. (John 14:15–20)

Read this promise carefully!

When we follow the Spirit's guidance, at times, events present dilemmas or what seem to be dead ends. This is where we found answers and actions that were unexpected or unexplainable—it was God's providential care! In some events, the need for a physical helper was provided by those we believe were God's angels, humans who may or may not have been aware they were God's angels.

We do not feel exempt from life's troubles, circumstances, and difficulties, but we have simple faith that God will deliver His obedient children from them all. If earthly life ends in a moment of difficulty, we will be eternally delivered into the presence of almighty God, our heavenly Father. In human terms, it is a win-win!

The record here is of those times when God used humans as His angels for the benefit of two believers. There were times that the personal belief as to the faith of those used was unknown.

God also uses other Christians to express His love for those who need providential help and care. Jesus introduced His disciples to this love. Unlike our world's references to love, God's love in and through believers is unique. It is expressed in the fellowship of the community of faithful in the church. For further understanding, God's love is clearly defined as a Christian attribute in 1 John and 1 Corinthians 13.

Nonbelievers used by God to bless believers may find satisfaction in doing something right. In most cases, unless told by the those blessed, nonbelievers do not know they are being used by God. They cannot understand our praise of God. Being detached from our lifestyle, they may believe we are somewhat unhinged when thanking them in the name of God.

The key to serving God is obedience. Max Lucado wrote, "Obedience pulls the ropes which rings the bells in heaven's belfries." This is a critical truth.

When the faithful are obedient to God, angels come to assist them in their difficult circumstances or events. When life has presented a dilemma for which there is no apparent solution or answer, God moves to implement His will, His plan, for the obedient. This is a clear and emphatic teaching of Jesus.

God makes plain His instructions for the believer's obedient conduct, daily attitudes, and actions in His Word. In his book, *My Utmost for His Highest*, Oswald Chambers explained on page one-fifty one the true meaning of obedience to God.

> The golden rule for spiritual understanding is not intellect but obedience. If a person wants scientific knowledge, intellectual curiosity is his guide; but if he wants insight into what Jesus Christ teaches, he can only get it by obedience. If things are dark to me, then I may be sure there is something I will not do. Intellectual darkness comes through ignorance; spiritual darkness comes because of something I do not intend to obey.

Obedience is the key to expecting the providence of God to be active in the life of a believer. Faith and obedience to God are fundamentals. We repeat: God places the Spirit of Jesus Christ, the Holy Spirit, in the believer's heart for the decisions of daily life.

Dr. David Jeremiah gave a clear and concise explanation of how the belief in God's providence helped shape our world.

> The word providence refers to the foreseeing, guiding, protecting, and rearranging by the hand of God on the history of the world and our personal lives. America's Founding Fathers leaned heavily on the doctrine of providence. According to several historians, George Washington's mother would read to him from Esther 4, emphasizing Mordecai's question to Esther: "Yet who knows whether you have come to the kingdom for such a time as this?" Young Washington absorbed the understanding that God controls events, placing us where and when He wants. As his life unfolded, Washington repeatedly spoke of providence. He talked about the "favorable interpositions" of God's

providence, the "ordering of a kind Providence," and "the hand of Providence" that spared America as a nation.

It is remarkable the same hand, which guides the course of history directs the circumstances of His children. Joseph was a man who yielded his life to the providential plan of God, and he became blessed and much used. God is in control of the tides of time; let Him also order the days of your life.

"A superintending Providence is ordering everything for the best—and, that in due time, all will end well." (George Washington, in a letter dated October 27, 1777)

CHAPTER 3

The Beginning

Let me live that I may praise You. (Psalm 119:175)

This is the record of the life experiences of John G. (Jack) Green and Mary Edna Burke Green. It reveals how they experienced the glory of God in a faith relationship with their loving Father. The references will be in the first person.

The nickname Jack came from a butcher friend of my father, whom we called Papa. At birth, mother, whom we called Mama, was informed by her doctor that her newborn baby had double pneumonia, for which there was no cure. One other doctor confirmed the diagnosis.

Mama had a live-in black woman named Anna who was with her during the birth of three of her four children. A middle brother, Billy, and a sister, Dorothy, and I were born in Birmingham. The older boy, Douglas, was born in Tennessee.

When Mama was bedfast after each birth of those born in Alabama, Anna became a cook and housekeeper. She would come as needed on other days. She was considered one of the family.

It was shortly after my birth that Anna heard the diagnosis of double pneumonia with no cure available. Mama told me how God brought a miracle. She said, "Anna became a doctor and a nurse." Here is how Anna nursed a baby with a critical illness in the first days of his life.

Anna did something she learned from the culture in which she was born. She made a mixture of some old-fashioned remedies for chest colds, flu, and breathing difficulties. With them, she bathed my chest and back. The medication was then put in a bandage and wrapped around my upper body.

Placing a rocking chair before the fireplace in the same room with Mama, Anna wrapped her patient in a light blanket and turned the critically ill child every few minutes. Anna's knee became a baby bed for two weeks or more. She sat before a blazing fire leaving the chair at baby's feeding time only for personal needs.

The result was not the one expected: God had a cure for double pneumonia. Mama spoke about how amazed the doctor was when he made a visit. He believed he had come to sign a death certificate; instead, he saw a healthy baby!

Looking back, we know it was the love and care of one who refused to accept a verdict of death for a baby whose life lay ahead. Anna trusted God to work through her. He had used her to perform a miracle! Anna was God's angel. This was His providential plan in action.

The example of Anna's faith in the Lord was evidence of how God can be trusted. It is an unforgotten, powerful influence on the boy who became a man. God used a faithful servant to make real His love and care, which is unavailable from any other source in our world.

Anna had a disabled daughter whom her sister cared for while she was away. Their home, on the outskirts of western Birmingham, had no running water in 1926.

To meet her need, Papa did a wonderful thing. He went to the office of the Birmingham Water Works, which was owned by stockholders, and bought shares of stock in the company in Anna's name. When he gave her the stock, he told her to take it to the Water Works office, lay it on the counter, and say, "I have come to petition for water lines to my home." She did, and the company responded positively. Anna had water lines laid to her home. God honors His believing angels.

Mama had Anna come one last time to be with our family. The oldest brother, Douglas, was in the navy. Billy, the middle brother, was in the army. My time for being called into the Army Air Corps in World War II lay ahead. It was a wonderful reunion; we shared a meal and childhood experiences with one we loved. Anna's care for us and her love for our family was etched on the minds of those she served.

Shortly after that day, beloved Anna went home to be with the Lord. Mama was asked to speak at her funeral. It was a time of weeping. God's blessing to us had gone to be with Him.

When we moved from the first home I could remember, it was from Woodlawn to Avondale in Birmingham. In that new home, we lived across the street from Avondale Park. It was a life-molding move with lessons that helped mold my life for the days ahead.

The neighborhood boys would meet at the park zoo, where there was an elephant named Miss Fancy and other animals from buffalos to monkeys. We knew every animal and gave each of them a personal name.

It was Miss Fancy who gave us thrills. After some time, she seemed to know us. Standing in admiration of our relationship to her, my group of friends would admire her every move. We knew many who would like to be her friend but never had the chance to see her.

As we stood admiring her one day, an older boy in our group put a wad of his chewing tobacco in a piece of cake and put it in Miss Fancy's snout. She stood for a long time as though deciding what she would do. Swinging her trunk widely, she stopped before the one who had given her the stuff, raised her trunk, and blew the stuff right in his face! While all the gang laughed, she seemed to be telling us clearly the difference between right and wrong and the inevitable result of wrongdoing.

Miss Fancy's caretaker would ride her and give her signals with his feet that she obeyed. One Sunday, he got drunk and rode her into the neighboring community of Avonwood. He had her lie down in the fork of two roads. It stopped cars and drew a crowd.

We would call her name, and she would turn her head as if she knew who was calling. The group thought we were something special!

Watching the drunk caretaker who was responsible for the scene made a lifetime impression that was evident as our group discussed the actions of the caretaker. His privilege was to be a caretaker of a wonderful animal, and we all thought that was a terrible abuse of that privilege. We had developed a great affection for an animal we considered our friend.

Our first real job was carrying water to baseball teams as they played their games in the park. The bucket was small with one water dipper from which everyone drank. The cost of the water was ten cents a game. About the sixth inning, we would ask the team captain for our money. That was a significant amount for a young boy or seemingly the same for a grown man as some did not want to pay. If they did not pay, we put someone behind the backstop fence. When a ball was fouled over the fence, the team would not get the ball back until someone paid the ten cents. It was business. We learned in simple ways how to live and work while learning how others should be treated. Honesty was needed for all of life.

One day, more than forty men were walking in the park. That raised a question. I asked Mama why there were so many grown men in the park, and she said they had nothing to do—no jobs. It was the Great Depression. Times were difficult for most of society.

When we were helping clean our house dugout, which we called a basement, something caught our eye—a trunk. If things of the past were in the trunk, I wanted to know what they were. As I raised the trunk lid, two things came into view that I would remember for a lifetime.

The first was a newspaper wrapped around long strands of black hair. It was beautiful but intriguing. I asked Mama about it later, and Mama said it was hers. She had to cut it because the doctor said it was causing her to have severe headaches. Never heard that before or since. This was the day a riddle was answered because we wondered why our mother wore her hair short, tailored almost like a man would cut his hair. A lifetime memory remains. She could not have looked more beautiful regardless of her hair.

The second item in the trunk gave a clue to Papa's life and habits. It was an envelope containing a check from the Avondale Bank. I opened it, and a check fell out. It had been made out to Papa, and it was for one cent! That raised questions and opened an understanding of our daddy like nothing before. I asked Mama about the check, and she said Papa had a large amount of savings in that bank. He had been wiped out financially when the bank went out of business.

Bankrupt bank! They were required to send checks resolving the account but not required to return the money. This was a result of the hardest financial times of a young country. It was a depression that lasted until the war was declared with Germany several years later.

Mama said Papa turned to drink more heavily than before after receiving that check. Later in life, I discussed this at work with my father-in-law, and he told me of the numerous self-inflicted deaths that took place among his customers' families. It was an event that shaped the lives of our nation's citizens including those in our family.

The Green family was busy. Rearing four children and taking care of a grandmother in the home meant that my parents and two brothers had to work. Mama's work as supervisor of activities at Avondale Park was demanding but enjoyable. All the sports were played in neighborhood gatherings in the park. Organizing and supervising events there were a tremendous responsibility. It also brought challenges.

The park had an amphitheater used by groups from around Alabama. Mama was responsible for all the arrangements for their meetings. Each year, there would be a pageant or a play presented in the open-air theater. Permanent rows of stone benches faced the stage, which had dressings rooms on each side. Mama organized and directed the pageants and plays.

One year, she called me into her room saying she needed my help. That was thrilling and puzzling. She most always just told me what she wanted me to do. To have a conference with her meant something important was on her mind.

Her play at the park for the year called for many girls. Then came the worst blow a young man could receive—Mama wanted to dress me as a girl! The thrill became a chill. What would our friends say about my playing the part of a girl?

Well, it happened. It was my deep wish that no one would recognize the Green boy, but they did! For several weeks, there were fights. Even close friends were making fun of the fact that I had been on stage dressed up as a girl. That was all I needed to start swinging at the one making the joke about the boy who became a girl.

Looking back, I see that it was a life-forming act. First, I had honored a loving mother's wish. I also knew that she had felt the pain of her son, which had been the reason for the confidential conference. It gave me a feeling of importance knowing I had met her needs.

The importance of defending against false pride became a lesson in what is essential in life. It was a lesson that taught a little fellow that criticism and mockery should be ignored rather than confronted. God's providence has a way of preparing one for His work. The many bruises were a good reminder and point of learning.

When I turned eight, my first job was with the Curtis Publishing Company selling the *Saturday Evening Post* and other magazines at the Continental Gin office in Avonwood and at the Jefferson County courthouse near downtown Birmingham. Mama later had a job at the courthouse café, where the company left the magazines. They were too numerous and bulky for an eight-year-old, but I learned that the number of magazines I sold each week was the largest in the area.

When the Child Labor Law became effective, carriers had to be twelve to get work permits. I had been building my route for two years, but a ten-year-old could not qualify. When a lawyer at the courthouse learned I was just ten, he told the Curtis Publishing Company, and his son got my route.

I told this to Matt Contri of C&M grocery, where a bunch of our gang worked when needed. I had an experience only God could have fashioned. When I shared with Matt about losing the magazine route, he began to put some items on the counter—small paper bags, a box of cocoa, five pounds of sugar, and a couple more items. "Take this home. Ask your Mama or sister, Dorothy, to make fudge. Pour it out on a sheet, cut it into equal pieces. Put five pieces in each bag. Sell it to your customers at the gin and the courthouse." It was an unexpected, stunning moment that would change the life of a little fellow. Matt Contri was God's angel helping to mold one of His children! The following seems unreal even in memory.

Telling Mama what Matt said stopped her for a moment. Then she said, "We'll make the candy and put it in a basket for you to carry. You can go to the gin on Friday afternoon. On Saturday morning, go to the courthouse before they get off at noon. You'll have to be patient to get the customers, but you'll be all right."

The providence of God is His personal plan for His children whom He loves! He uses designated angels when circumstances reveal a need. That was never plainer than the day He used Matt Contri to help a very disappointed ten-year-old who thought he had lost two years of hard work. Without work, there would be no way I could help with family finances and have some spending money.

The workers at the courthouse went home on Saturdays at noon. My spiel was to tell them to put the candy in a drawer and eat it one piece at a time with their lunches, which they brought from home. It worked! I took every magazine customer from the new boy! It was either a nickel for a magazine or my candy, which was all they could afford. This seems odd today, but it gives thought as to the serious times of that day.

With the candy route, God began to fashion a life of one saved from death when born to a life of service to Him. Very little or nothing at the time was known about the Bible or the Holy Spirit of God. When God has a plan for someone's life and that person is willing, it is put in place one day, one activity, one learning experience at a time.

On a Saturday morning when I was walking down the hall of the courthouse, Judge Abernathy of the Court of Misdemeanors called out, "Bo!" That was his name for the candy boy. I answered his summons, and he said, "When do you get through with your sales route?" I said,

"About ten o'clock, sir." "When you're finished, come to my chambers," he said. In shock, I said, "Yes sir!"

Going into Judge Ab's chamber was a new experience. He gave a word of thanks for my coming and said, "Bo, I want you to stand on the bench with me every Saturday. I'll show you how to call the court to order and why I want you with me." That was stunning and frightening. Judge Ab did not know it, but we will see that God was using him to fashion the life of one of His children. This was God's angel at work!

While opening court with words taught by Judge Ab, I smacked the gavel on the bench with a resounding stamp of authority. Court attendees became very quiet though they were puzzled to see a young boy standing by the judge.

When two men appeared for trial after an auto accident, it became clear to me why the judge wanted someone with him. He had miniature cars in the bench drawer. Judge Ab wanted the small cars taken from his desk drawer and placed according to the report of the accident in their positions when it occurred. With the little cars in place, he would ask of the events causing the accident. If one told him he had had the right of way, he would be automatically guilty. Judge Ab thought such a remark meant the person had taken advantage of the privilege. He was a pragmatic judge.

When gamblers or bootleggers would appear for trial, it was like a theater show or a scene from television. If it was a gambling trial, Judge Ab would ask for the dice from the drawer to be given to the accused. Permission was given for the accused to kneel and throw the dice against the bench.

Judge Ab would say, "Roll boxcars or two aces and I'll let you go. Throw sevens and you're going to jail. Only crooks throw sevens with house dice." The waiting witnesses or friends would roar in laughter. "Court comes to order," was the personal shout as the gavel smacked the bench.

These and many more life situations made clear to me matters that would have never been clear otherwise. It was a tremendous lesson from one who seemed to take me under his personal care having heard how the magazine route had been taken away from me.

When I was talking to the judge in his chambers one time, I asked about a man who sat with a pencil and pad at every trial. The judge said, "He's the court reporter. Using shorthand, he writes every word I say and every word spoken by the attorneys, witnesses, and the defendants. At home, he types them up and brings them to me."

I thought of the great times we had while on the bench; it seemed to me that court reporting was a great job. I told the judge that, and his reply opened the door to a new high school venture; he said I would have to take shorthand and typing classes.

The decision I made that day changed my life. I entered Woodlawn High School at age thirteen and signed up for typing and shorthand; I wanted a career as a court reporter. My older brothers wanted to disown their little brother for taking those classes as no other boys were taking them. The girls in each class seemed to like it and offered to do the homework for the new boy. Previously, Mama had given me a chance to learn how to face criticism and mockery, so I was prepared.

Typing came naturally while shorthand took effort, but later, I realized God had been at work and had given me the ability to take shorthand and use a typewriter.

Mama's mother lived with us and handled the housekeeping and cooking for the family while Mama was working. Evening meals, which Grandmama prepared, were the best. Attendance at the meal was required unless we were excused for work or a personal need. Those were great times as everyone could share what had taken place during the day.

Mama handled discipline in the family. On a rare occasion, Papa taught all of us a lesson. Douglas sat next to Papa at the table. One night when we were having turnip greens, Douglas sniffed them before eating them, and Papa did something we had never experienced; he smacked Douglas with the back of his hand. Sitting on a stool, his favorite seat at the table, Douglas landed on the floor against the wall. Papa told him to get up and come stand by him.

"Young man," he said, "you got hit because you were insulting your mother and grandmother. If you were thinking they put something unfit to eat on the table, you should excuse the offering to have it on your plate. Never put food from this table to your nose again."

Later, the three of us not affected discussed it. We thought it was a hard way to learn a lesson, but we would never forget it.

Grandmama was a politically minded woman. She would stand on a downtown Birmingham street handing out cards for those running for political offices if they paid her transportation to downtown Birmingham and gave her meal money.

We shared a bedroom in early life. A love of history was formed as she told the experiences of her parents and grandparents during the Civil War. When extra money was earned above that which went into the jar Mama kept on top of the icebox for family use, Grandmama would keep it for me. She was a stingy banker. If my request was for fifty cents, she would give me twenty-five. It was a severe lesson about the value of money and how to use it, but later in life, it was a valuable lesson in our ministry.

When Mama was at work, Grandmama monitored our dress and manners. It was a personal learning experience with deep love expressed and shared by both. With a fond look back, I realize it was God's hand fashioning how we should look and act.

It is not always a crisis when God chooses to use His angels, and the following is a noteworthy example. Grandmama was God's angel preparing her grandson for a life of service and respect for all people.

The funeral for Grandmama Parker was in their family church in Pulaski, Tennessee. She had walked the town getting donations for the purchase of a new piano for the church, which was played for the first time at her burial. Her funeral was the first and hardest for a young preacher who was burying one he loved dearly.

In our community, everyone knew everyone else. We played together, ate together, and shared life. Mr. Shannon, founder and owner of Shannon Cycle Company in downtown Birmingham, lived near us. He had a cow that he kept in a stable behind his home. Mama would milk the cow for a share of the milk, which she made into butter. His daughter was disabled from birth. Playing games with her was a lesson in taking care of the disadvantaged. She was family, and she had our love and care.

My sister, Dorothy, and I attended the Avondale Methodist Church Sunday school. Mr. Shannon was a leader in the church. When we stayed for worship, he would ask us to sit with him. That was an honor!

Mama did not go to church as Papa was drinking heavily. He would go to work looking like a million dollars but come home looking like he had been in a fight. It was not pleasant on those nights. Mama's tending to a drunk husband taught us much about keeping a family together and the sacredness of marriage.

The older brothers were in school or working. Mama needed her youngest son's help in wringing water from the clothes and especially the overalls. She washed them in our backyard in a large tub over a fire and hung them to dry on a line that stretched across the backyard.

I was helping Mama one wash day when the phone rang. Our phone was on a line with an operator, who would ring for the caller. Sitting on the floor near the back door, I heard the conversation. When the call was finished, I saw that Mama was visibly upset. "Mama, what is it? What's wrong?"

She was quiet for a long time before she said, "Honey, it was a call from a woman who had seen your father when he came home after drinking. She thought I was complaining about him when she asked me how it was going, and I told her it was very hard. She didn't know I was talking about washing the overalls."

Mama had become disturbed when the woman asked, "Why don't you just take the children and leave him?" Mama had told her, "I married him for better or worse. In the better, God has given us four wonderful children. In the worse, I trust God to make Walter a better man." She hung up without saying goodbye.

Later, when I was pastoring a church near home, my parents came to hear my sermons. To God's glory, Papa heard many sermons that told of God's forgiveness and love. Later, when he was ill, he told the family of his baptism in a Tennessee river as a young man. He had strayed, but hearing my sermons lifted a burden from his heart.

While I was pastor at Inwood Baptist Church in Raleigh, North Carolina, Papa came to stay for a few weeks. One Sunday, our six-year-old son was being quite loud in his childish behavior. After church, two men were discussing his behavior. "That boy, if he was mine, would get a whipping, and he deserves it." Papa heard them and said, "Gentlemen, you're talking about my grandson. It would be appreciated if you acted like godly men!" He had come full circle from the early days that had marked him, Mama, and our family. We attributed it to the one who loved our daddy, prayed for him, and saw God's glory.

When we were children, the community fashioned our lives. When Papa was able to buy a Crosley radio, the entire neighborhood knew about it. On certain nights when *The Lone Ranger* or some other popular program came on, we would have a house full. Neighbors came to sit, talk, and drink coffee until the station went off the air. There was no gossip, arguing, or debating politics; it was just a time of sitting, talking, listening, and loving. A blessed time! Neighborhood children came with their parents, and we looked forward to those times together.

When I was twelve, our family moved to nearby Avonwood, a place with a drug store, two grocery stores, and a dry-cleaning shop. The Continental Gin main office was there. We boys occasionally worked at the grocery stores and the drug store. It was there that we met Matt Contri, the grocery owner whom God used in my life.

Our love of baseball and football got us out to Avondale Park. Around the corner from our house was the home of Oscar Cagle, a marvelous athlete who was three years our elder. His father was among the blessed during the Great Depression; he had a job as a railroad conductor. Eating at their home was a new experience for us. The first time they prayed before eating made a great impression on me, who had never done that before.

Oscar became our boyhood friend and my personal idol. Our

daughter Jackie was given his middle name, Lee. Of all childhood friends, he was the one who had the greatest influence on me.

I was double-promoted twice in grammar school, but that had consequences when I entered high school. I had played sandlot football and wanted to play the sport in high school, but my size and weight precluded that.

I thought that the next best thing would be cheerleading, but no boy had ever been a Woodlawn High cheerleader. Being the first was more than a novelty. Yelling and leading cheers was a thrilling experience, and it was great to be with all those girls of course.

Later, having had enough of that experience, I sought the job of the team's assistant equipment manager. I did not have that position for long, but it was fun traveling with the team.

During our high school years, Oscar and I had an afternoon newspaper route when there was no football practice. We continued the job in the summer. We rode a bicycle together to throw the papers. He had the stronger legs and pedaled the bike. Riding on the bike bar gave me time to roll the papers. I handed them off to Oscar, who threw them on the customers' porches.

While on our route one day, Oscar asked if I could come to church with him that night, a Wednesday. I asked why he would go to church on a Wednesday night, and he said they were having a revival, something I was not familiar with. Nevertheless, the request was an honor; going to church with Oscar was another chance to be with my best friend.

As we sat in the balcony of the Avondale Baptist Church, the Word of God came clearly from Dr. A Hamilton Reid, executive director of Alabama Baptist. He sounded like an Englishman at times, but his words were clear enough to penetrate my young heart.

At the close of the sermon, he asked those who felt a need for God and would live for Him and serve Jesus Christ to come down and take his hand. Those words hit home. I never tried to parse their full meaning, but the urge became a need that called for action.

While going down the stairs, I had a calm mind and heart though it was a new experience. The old door to the main area was stuck.

With a great pull, it flew open for a flight down the aisle to speak to the evangelist.

I took the minister's hand. He asked my name and why I had come to the front. "Sir, what you said is not all that clear to me, but I believe in God and want Jesus to clean my heart and make me His Christian." He asked me to bow my head, and he begin praying that I would ask God for forgiveness and promise to live for Him. A twelve-year-old became a believer in Christ that day. Glory! It was a life-changing experience. Dr. Reid was God's angel at work that evening. God used him for my eternal salvation, and there was singing in heaven!

The walk across the park to home was shorter than at any time of my life. The dark of night did not frighten me. The air was still. I felt a genuine joy in my new life! It was a memorable and life-changing night.

Mama was waiting for me; she wanted to know about the service. She was a loving, kind, and very intelligent mother. When she heard about the sermon and my response, prayer, and the feeling of God in my heart, she wept softly. Mama's childhood family worshiped when services were held at their rural church in Pulaski. She knew what her youngest son had experienced. I have chills remembering that.

We knelt before her to listen for her response. She told of her own experience as a child, which she had never shared with us. She took my face in her hands and said, "It's a wonderful thing to be a Christian. It won't be easy. You'll learn that God will be with you in a very special way. But remember, as it feels so good, a life lived for the Lord is for His glory."

Later, she remembered that night when I became the interim pastor for two years at her Cumberland Presbyterian Church. We worshiped together and remembered how it had all started. Her faith had kept our family together. It was the seed that grew by God's hand and providence into a tree of life.

God had used Oscar to make it all happen. His simple invitation to attend a church opened the door for the Holy Spirit to do His work in me. Salvation is an act of God's love for sinning humanity. Oscar joined those beautiful angels who touched and guided a young life. It was God's providence, His plan.

Oscar served in the US Army Air Corps as a pilot commander of a flight squadron. On a mission over Germany, his wingman's plane was in trouble. A German fighter plane was on his tail ready to blow the plane out of the air. Oscar called to warn him. The wingman had no ammunition. Oscar did a wing-over hitting the German midplane. Both went down in flames. Neither pilot survived. This was evidence of why Oscar was our hero. He died for a fellow airman. He would have done the same for me. He died as he lived proving that the love of God is the strongest force on earth.

CHAPTER 4

A Life-Changing Day

I will strengthen you and help you. (Isaiah 41:10)

On December 7, 1941, my brothers were caddying at the Highland Park Golf Course, and they had permitted me to tag along; they had not done that frequently. I considered it a joy to be included, but missing Sunday school was something that would be a bother later in life.

On the golf course, we received some shocking news. As we approached the green of the first hole, which was near a street, a fast car approached our area. The woman driver slammed on the brakes and jumped out of the car. She was shouting, "They just bombed Pearl Harbor! The Japanese just bombed Pearl Harbor!"

We were startled and confused. We turned to each other and asked, "Where's Pearl Harbor? Why would someone want to bomb it?" Of course, we later got our answer in the newspaper and on the radio, but for the rest of that day, we could only wonder.

The next morning, Woodlawn High's principal called everyone to the auditorium to hear a radio address by President Roosevelt; we heard him say, "This is a day which will be remembered in infamy." We did not know the full meaning of all he said, but we got the first inkling in our hearts that we were in a full-scale national emergency.

That was the opening of World War II for the United States. That act by the Japanese gave birth to life-changing circumstances that affected every life in the auditorium, every life in America, no exceptions.

It would be only a few months before my seventeenth birthday and high school graduation. Then there would be an opportunity for me to enlist in the military.

It has never been clear why the US Army Air Corps was my first choice. It may have been the news that they were signing seventeen-year-olds or the influence of Oscar, who was impressed by the air corps. My enlistment was for pilot training and combat service. Time in service would begin on or after my eighteenth birthday. While I was a senior in high school, the war was in full force.

The Bechtel-McCone-Parsons Corporation had begun building a bomber-modification plant at the Birmingham airport. They hired me at age seventeen to work in its mailroom, which later became a job in the security department.

Mama, who had been a telephone operator in Nashville before she married, applied for a telephone switchboard job at the same plant. We worked from four to twelve each evening. No transportation was available at the late hour, so we had a four-mile walk home each night.

It was a real experience being with Mama on that walk home. She used the time to share her teachings about how God wanted His children to live. She was a great teacher! Some of the experiences she shared about her trials and how she handled them inspired me as I was maturing.

After I graduated, the director of the modification project called me to his office. He spoke of the difficulty the government was having in finding a qualified stenographer for the work in a project in Tennessee. Having heard of my training to be a stenographer, he asked if the military had indicated when my call for service was coming. I told him I had to be eighteen or older to be called up for military service, and that was several months in the future in my case. He asked if I would take the job at Oak Ridge, Tennessee, to work on the Manhattan Project. I later learned that it was a top-secret military project.

Once again, looking back, we saw the work of the hand of God. Our sister's husband, Brannon Jones, had taken a job as a boilermaker at the same project. They had a baby then and bought a house trailer to take to Tennessee so they could be together on his new job. The trailer was parked in a lot not far from Oak Ridge. It was a pleasant surprise and joy to be able to be to stay with them! After their offer, word came there were no rooms available in Oak Ridge or any nearby town. When God arranges the circumstances, He leaves nothing to chance!

The work assignment at Oak Ridge was different from anything known to most Americans. Concrete sections the size of motel rooms were joined in rows. Pipes that went through the walls of every cell block brought fluids to instruments in each unit, and they needed calibrating and adjusting. That was the work of an instrumentation engineer, and there was only one instrumentation engineer in the United States, a professor at MIT in Boston. He was not available for the project. Mr. Raymond Altoff, a Swede, was smuggled into the country to work on the highly secret project. Sweden was a neutral country in the war, but Russia heavily monitored it.

The J. A. Jones Construction Company was building the project. They hired me, a seventeen-year-old from Alabama, to be the stenographer and assistant to the new Swedish engineer.

The Manhattan Project became known as the place the first US atomic bomb was made for military use. The instrumentation engineer's job was to calibrate the instruments in each cell to make them suitable to process chemicals needed for the project. Mr. Altoff had to have known the purpose of the project. He knew the exact final reading for the different sets of items in each cell. After calibrating the instruments, he would give instructions to change the blueprints to the correct settings. That was demanding work for a seventeen-year-old; the specifications were critical for the completion of the project.

It rained almost every day of work at the project. There were no concrete walks or accommodations. After wading in mud up to our knees, we needed to take baths before touching the blueprints, which were in a secluded room at the central construction office. There were notes to be translated, typed, and put on the engineer's desk for approval before becoming permanent records. That was the work of a seventeen-year-old stenographer who never knew of the purpose until months after leaving the project.

Swedish is drastically different from English, and there was no time for lessons. Becoming a tutor in English was a new experience for me. For the two of us, communication was tough, but Mr. Altoff became a friend and a good student of English. Our time together was a unique experience. What I learned about communication with him at Oak Ridge became a blessing when I worked years later in Korea with non-English speaking people. The providence of God has many aspects that defy logic or understanding when they occur.

After I finished with the settings and changes for the completed units, my urge to join the military was strong. I left the Manhattan Project and waited for a call to service while doing some short-time work.

During high school days, the three Green boys worked for Mr. James Dickson, who had the franchise for the sale of food and soft drinks at football games at Legion Field in Birmingham. He also had a contract to provide food and other items for troop trains at the Birmingham Terminal station. Mr. Dickson said he could use my help at the train station if the seven p.m. to seven a.m. shift was not too long. I readily accepted the job.

While I was working at the station, God revealed the cost of war to one about to serve his country. I served box lunches to wounded troops on trains coming through Birmingham and headed to hospitals. That was a sobering experience for someone about to enter the war.

One evening while I was working the cigarette and candy shop in the train station, a couple asked for a pack of cigarettes. I was busy stocking shelves, so I just put a pack on the counter without even looking at them. I said over my shoulder, "That'll be twenty-five cents."

When I did not hear any money hit the counter, I said sharply, "That'll be twenty-five cents!" again. I turned and looked at my customers and was shocked. The woman was fumbling in her purse and apologizing for taking up my time. The man standing beside her was in a dress military uniform, but there were no arms in his sleeves. They were gone. With a stammering, apologetic, tear-filled voice, I said, "There'll be no charge."

From that day forward, I never took for granted the price our men and women paid in wars. God gave me a shock when He showed me how many people lived the remainders of their lives with bodies maimed and battered. I learned the price of freedom. That lesson was etched on my young heart forever.

God's strength comes to those who are in need. I shared this tear-stained experience from the pulpit in the years ahead; it inspired those whose loved ones were mangled and sacrificed to keep us free.

Chapter 5

Off We Go ...

...what we shall be has not been made known...
1 John 3:2

The train station job ended when the US Army Air Corps called me to basic training in Biloxi, Mississippi. There, I learned to march, shoot, eat, and sleep while being obedient to the discipline of superiors and military life.

After six weeks of basic training, it became clear to me that there was unfinished business I had to take care of before the call to active duty.

Mr. Dickson, who had the terminal station concession, also owned a swimming pool, Cascade Plunge in the eastern section of Birmingham. In the summer of our junior year in high school, he needed some workers. The work was in the locker room with occasional duty as a lifeguard when a regular lifeguard needed a break.

On a beautiful day, a group of young girls came for a swim. It was our day to work in relief for a pool guard. The girls gathered in the shallow end of the pool, which provided a good place to get to know them. That desire needed fulfilling.

I swam out to get acquainted with them, and I thought the smallest girl in the group looked beautiful. As I thought about how to meet her, an impulse to do something odd took over me. I swam underwater, came up behind her, put my hands on her shoulders, and forced her underwater. She came up with a wild look in her eyes—she was incensed! A foolish young boy attempted an apology and played it off as just a friendly act. She was not impressed.

Making her acquaintance came easier after I apologized two or three times for my initial foolishness, and our being about the same height made her somewhat comfortable. We became friends, and we played water games for the rest of the day. It was pleasant. In fact, it was joyful!

On that day, a future airman met the girl of his dreams. Mary Edna Burke became my steady girlfriend. She knew there would be a call from the military for me, so our dating became rather frequent.

On our last date before I left for full-time service a year later, she accepted an engagement ring. God had led me to a lifetime partner. Ours became a life of love to each other and service to our Lord, which took us to twenty-two countries and lasted seventy-two years.

During my basic training in Biloxi, the first thing I learned was, "No soldier will be permitted to have a pass to leave the post while in basic training." But I wanted to marry Mary Edna Burke, so I made an appeal to the adjutant of the unit. As I had expected, his reply was, "No passes." But in a very indirect way, he was told about a certain man-sized hole in the fence near our barracks that just happened to lead straight to the train station. The wedding had been planned, and the need for the pass was urgent!.

The adjutant sat back in his chair and put his hand on his chin in deep thought before he slowly said, "I'm granting you a pass, son, because of all you have told me, but no one in the unit must be told about it, now or ever! There will be a heavy penalty if I hear of it."

On a rainy Saturday night in West End Baptist Church in Birmingham, Alabama, Mary Edna became the bride of Airman Private Green. The honeymoon was in a local hotel. Her girlfriends did their best to make the night miserable, which was impossible for two who loved each other beyond their understanding.

We were both quite young. I had been out of school and had worked for two years before being called to active service. Mary Edna, my age, finished high school at a normal age and time.

Upon completion of basic training, all the guys in our unit were excited. We waited anxiously to know which pilot training base would be our assignment. Shortly afterward, we heard our captain say, "Gentlemen, we have enough pilots, but we do need some good gunners who can shoot a machine gun straight from a bomber." We were then US Army Air Corps gunners!

Gunnery training was in Las Vegas, Nevada. On the coolest day, the temperature would reach a hundred degrees. The commander ordered all training to stop at eleven in the morning and resume at four in the afternoon.

Before we flew, we had to undergo physicals. I weighed about a hundred and twenty-eight, and my blood pressure always registered on the low side. The doctor who took my blood pressure said, "Son, your pressure is too low for flying. It could be fatal."

At that moment, he was called to the telephone in another room. The door standing open was my answer to the negative report. Going behind the door and jumping up and down on one foot and then the other for ten minutes was all that was needed.

When the doctor came back, I asked him to take my blood pressure again. He did, and he said, "Alabama, what in the h*** have you done?" I just grinned. The doctor said, "You passed, but you're not going to walk back to your barracks in this heat." He called for a jeep. It was a great ride for an army private.

After I finished gunnery training, I was assigned to an airbase in Lincoln, Nebraska. The planes there were used for training crews for combat. Many incidents took place in that sector that were never reported to the public.

We never looked forward to night-flying training missions; there was always a chance for an untoward event, but the providence, plan, and care of God for one of his own was active one night.

The captain of our plane that night had been told by operations not to fly around or over Omaha as the weather was turbulent. As I sat in the middle gunner's compartment for takeoff, the word came clear through the earphones: "Captain, you need to change your flight plan." He ignored the warning; there was no new flight plan filed with operations. We took off, and I was shocked to realize we were headed for Omaha!

We never knew why the captain had ignored operations, but it was strikingly clear why the warning had been given. Near Omaha, the weather was not fit for aircraft. The tail gunner's position was abandoned as the plane bounced a hundred or more feet up and down with each gust of wind.

The turbulence blew the plane off the flight plan. Shortly, the captain filed a new flight plan with the control network. He was then told to find his own field for landing. Everything in the area was under a weather watch and was accepting no planes.

There was turmoil in our plane. All were asking on the intercom where we were headed. It was tremendously stressful. The only available landing strip where no weather would hinder us was in Missouri, the opposite direction of the training target. It seemed the entire Midwest was experiencing the same winds and weather.

It was a near-death situation with the turbulence and winds as strong as those in a tornado. To add to the stress, our pilot and crew were quite young with little experience in turbulent weather.

It was near midnight. There were no accommodations for airmen on the post of the airport that would accept our landing. No beds or food. Canteens were closed. But sleeping on the floor with a boot for a pillow was better than being blown into the Atlantic Ocean or a mountain range.

It will always be a night to remember! By God's grace and mercy, we lived to write about God's providential care in ways beyond understanding.

While we were stationed in Nebraska, on some days, no flights were made. A pocket Bible, a gift from a loving father-in-law, became my steady reading material. All the guys saw the time I spent on my bunk reading that little book.

One was a soldier from North Carolina, Charlie Pipes. Knowing there would be several days off duty, Charlie asked if I would join him in getting some part-time work. Without too much thought and no prayer, I agreed. He said he was going to ask if there was work available at a farmer's feed store. He did, and they hired us to come in each afternoon to prepare feed for the cattle.

On one afternoon, we were told to pitch the hay stored in a boxcar pulled up beside the store. We used hay forks to throw the hay onto a conveyor leading into an opening on the second floor. The hay was green, dried alfalfa.

We worked for two or more hours. I glanced over at Charlie and could not see anything but his eyes. Everything else—face, neck, hands, arms—was covered in green alfalfa. I asked him how I looked, and he said, "Can't see nothing but your eyes!" That was enough. We asked for our pay and where we could take a shower.

The next few hours were a nightmare. Charlie went to a bar alone. I saw him staggering down the street later; he had been drinking heavy. A military police captain stopped Charlie and said, "Soldier, you better catch a bus to the post. If I see you again, you'll be going to the guardhouse." Charlie said, "Yes sir!"

That meant nothing to him. He stepped into another bar. When he came out, I decided it was time to take him to the bus station. His clothes looked like he had been fighting. His cap was on sideways. His speech was heavily slurred. We looked down the street and saw the MP captain standing on the corner. It was two in the morning. We were in front of an all-night theater. We bought tickets and ducked into the theater. We sat, and Charlie immediately went to sleep and started snoring loudly.

We sat through that movie twice. It was starting for the third time when Charlie finally came back to life. We took the bus back to the post and barely made roll call.

A few days later, Charlie asked if we could read God's Word together. That had never happened before. The reading was from the Gospels, but there was little understanding of what was read.

Finishing one reading, Charlie began to tell me about his troubles. He was engaged, but his fiancée told him she would not marry him until he stopped drinking, and he was a heavy drinker. Charlie thought he should turn to God to rid him of his habit. He wanted to make the change because he was in love.

We read scripture several times aloud, no discussion. It seemed the message was clear without explanation. It must have had an eternal impact on Charlie.

Some years later, my wife and I made a trip to Charlie's home in North Carolina. He had married his loved one, and they had several children. It was a joyous reunion! We thought about the days we had spent flying and how God had kept us safe.

Charlie was a Christian believer. He had given up drinking shortly after his time in the service. He was a good husband with a good job and a godly wife and family.

It was clear to both of us—reading the pocket Bible given to me by my father-in-law was God's way for the seed to be sown for a life that would honor Him. To God's glory, a young, biblically uneducated believer became an angel to a needy soldier. God's providential care is for every soul, and believers praise Him for it.

Charlie was the first of many of my personal acquaintances whom God would claim as His Spirit-led. It was not by knowledge but by a redeemed heart that knew God had something better for all of us! It was wonderful evidence that anyone can be God's angel for the needy!

CHAPTER 6

Beyond Understanding

... neither are your ways My ways. (Isaiah 55:8)

The time I spent in the air corps was deeply satisfying. It may have been the freedom and joy of flying in God's clouds free of earthly restraints. I felt the satisfaction of serving my country. For these and other reasons, I extended my enlistment in the air corps by a year. As frequently happens, decisions are made that by hindsight seem foolish. Shortly after I reenlisted, I was sent to Fort Jackson, South Carolina. The base there needed someone who could type, and that meant that I, a corporal, had no more flying time. The assignment office was commanded by a very competent major with whom I developed a great relationship though it proved to be for only a short time.

During one of my off days, the major sent me a note; he wanted me to pack up for a new assignment at Bolling Field, Washington, DC. The suddenness of the change was somewhat disturbing. The major's note said nothing about the nature of the assignment, but I thought it certainly had to be something special because I, a corporal, would be flown there.

It had begun to rain when the B-26 aircraft arrived. The pilot, a colonel, came into the office to collect his passenger. After I identified myself to him, he said he could not fly as the plane was not equipped with night-flying instruments in inclement weather with little or no lights on the runway. He said he would see me in the morning, and he left for a motel. I slept on a wood bench and had nothing to eat.

The next morning, the weather was worse, but it cleared up by ten, and we took off for Washington. When we landed, a colonel met our plane. He was greatly agitated about our being late. He told the pilot, "You got the right man here, but it's too late. His flight has left."

Having heard that, I figured the assignment had been filled. I said to the colonel, "Sir, if my flight has left, would you permit me to go over to Flight OPS and see if I can get a deadhead flight back to Fort Jackson?" I realized that my wife and our baby were unaware I was no longer in South Carolina. It would have been pleasant to get back there.

The colonel's answer was quick and to the point: "No. I have another need, and your skills will be good for it. I'll take you over to the Pentagon and fill you in."

That was a shock. "Sir, could you tell me what flight was missed?" The reply took my breath away: "It was a flight to China with General Marshall. He's going to set up a new program, which will be known as the Lend-Lease Program, to help the countries that have been decimated by the war."

Once again, the Lord had intervened! Bad weather meant missing a flight to China. I hoped the new assignment would be better than the one I had missed. I learned later that the China assignment lasted years.

The Pentagon was another grand experience. The colonel led me up and down the corridors of that marvelous structure answering my questions as we walked to his office. He told me that my new assignment would be with the Navy Department, which seemed a strange place for an army airman. But when the colonel informed me of the work I was to do, it made sense.

The navy was sending ninety-five ships to the Bikini Atoll in the Pacific. The navy would drop an atomic bomb there and observe the damage to the ships. Later, there would be an underwater explosion to see if that damaged the vessels.

My assignment was to be an aide to General Blakelock, a logistics expert. I didn't know what the word *logistics* meant, so the colonel said that the general would be responsible for the proper materials being available for the fleet and the test.

My work in the Navy Department required long hours, but I was able to bring my wife to Washington for a few weeks; her mother watched Jackie, our daughter, a beautiful little redhead.

There was one notable incident. The navy captain assigned to the work in the Navy Department asked me to get coffee for him rather than stop his navy personnel from their work. That happened twice each morning.

To reach the coffee area, I had to cross an open breezeway leading to a second-story stairway that led to the office of the Secretary of the Navy. On one occasion when I was going for coffee, the door was blocked. I peered through the glass door and glimpsed President Harry Truman! That was one day the request from the navy captain for coffee was truly a blessing. Few have ever seen a president up close and personal. While it was not personal, it was truly up close.

Late one afternoon when the office crew was gone for the day, I asked the general, "Sir, if you will pardon me, I have a request." He nodded. With much hesitation, I said, "Sir, this is a request for a reassignment." The general seemed sincerely shocked. "You want what? Why?"

I told him about my having to get coffee for the captain even though that had allowed me to see President Truman. The general assured me that my coffee duties would stop and asked me if I needed anything else.

"Yes sir, there is another matter. I hesitate to mention it, but to do my work as you need it, I want to tell you what has upset me. Sir, your language when talking to me is rough. It is very difficult to concentrate on your orders when you speak so disrespectfully of our Lord among other things."

There was a long, quiet, and somewhat frightening pause. His reply was short and to the point. "Son, you're the first one to ever mention my language to me. In fact, I'm not aware of what you mentioned, but I know it's true. I'll pay attention to what I'm saying from now on. There will be no transfer."

My relationship with the general changed dramatically. He was more polite and quieter in my presence; he did not curse even when others were with me. When I left the assignment, I received a beautiful, handwritten note from him that expressed his appreciation for my work. It was a personal thanks for my help on the project. It seemed to be a subtle reference to the request concerning his language.

This confirmed those readings from the pocket Bible that told of keeping the Lord's name sacred. It was God's way of revealing the power of obedience to Him in daily life. The Lord had blessed our time together.

CHAPTER 7

Complete Circle

He has rescued us from the dominion of darkness.
(Colossians 1:3)

It is amazing how life's circumstances and events can bring you full circle. The following is a reference to the life of an eyewitness to world-changing activity.

On the atomic bomb test Able in the Bikini Lagoon, the first bomb to be dropped was to determine by eyewitness the damage to the ninety-five naval vessels when it exploded above them.

The flagship of Joint Task Force One was the USS *Mount McKinley*, with Admiral William H. P. Blandy in command. For Test Able, Secretary of the Navy James Forrestal came aboard. As a recorder for the Navy Department of a visual report of the damage, my place was to stand between the admiral and the secretary of the navy on the flag deck. Our full view of the ships would make an evaluation of damage easier. It was an exciting time for a young soldier.

We had worked long hours in very hot weather. Our quarters on the flagship for Operation Crossroad had a speaker directly over the bunks on the wall or bulkhead as the navy called it. I received calls from the general for notes to be taken as late as two in the morning; the boss never slept! It was strange but exciting.

On test day, an admiral from the tech ship anchored nearby came aboard. There was a small telescope-type instrument on the rail of the flag deck. He was to look through the scope while dictating the visual damage, information the navy wanted.

While the plane was approaching the lagoon, the admiral told me to look through the instrument, an icaroscope. He said, "You can get your facts with this instrument. You can see the explosion and damage through it." The visual observer who was to dictate to me found another spot to watch the explosion.

Prior to the test, Admiral Blandy moved the flagship back a few hundred feet for extra safety. The B-29 Superfortress, *Dave's Dream*, dropped the bomb, which missed the target by over two thousand feet.

The scope made the sun look like the moon; that made it possible for me to look at the damage to the vessels without protecting my eyes, and it made the cloud after the explosion look like a benign mushroom. The heat from the explosion came with a force of a warm wind that pushed me back several feet, but my vision was not impaired by the heat or the force. The most difficult thing was to remember the mission. Few people have witnessed an atomic explosion and lived to record it. It was our personal responsibility to witness and record. It was done.

The next few days were hazy. The notes I made of the damage seen by the naked eye on a scope were included in the official report.

Then the bottom dropped out. Due to the heat, the long hours of work, and little time for eating, I was taking a beating. Within two weeks, my health became the center of attention. No one knew how to diagnose the problem of my loss of weight and stamina.

There was to be another atomic test. The recorder would not be available. The ship's doctor ordered total bed rest for me, but the longer I did that, the worse my condition became. He finally said, "Young man, you're going back to the States."

I received that message with mixed emotions. General Blakelock had become a dear friend as well as a mentor and commander. The decision almost drove me to tears. He later expressed his feelings in a letter, and my impression of our relationship was confirmed.

The navy sent a seaplane to take me to a nearby island that had an airbase, where I was put on a flight in my sick condition. Nurses cared for me and others on board; our destination was a hospital in Virginia. The illness and the long flight had taken their toll. Several doctors came to look at me, who had in their minds a strange illness. When they learned of my exposure to atomic radiation, their interest peaked. Several asked me questions and checked my vitals while seeming to be very unsettled. The doctors told me they had never seen anyone with my symptoms; they weren't able to make a diagnosis, so they decided to fly me to a hospital in Augusta, Georgia.

When I got there, I went through the same routine, and my condition puzzled the doctors there too. They had one unanimous diagnosis—"This soldier has bad blood!" While that may be a simplification of the matter, no doctor told me or wrote down that I was suffering from radiation exposure. Many high-ranking members of the military met as a panel to discuss that fact. After two years, they decided that our ship had been out of the radiation exposure range, but they compensated those involved in the tests who developed several types of cancer.

Having no experience or training that spoke to my needs, the doctors settled on the obvious. One time, while I was helping General Blakelock move heavy boxes on a transport ship while looking for elements of the bomb he was to assemble, I saw a box falling toward the general. I caught the box but displaced my shoulder. That damage was evident to the doctors.

Later, one doctor wanted to take part of my shin bone and fuse it with the injured shoulder. We agreed, but on second thought, that didn't seem right. This conclusion was confirmed by a fellow soldier who had the procedure and ended up with infections in his leg and arm.

When the doctor returned to set up the operation, he received my request to stabilize my arm in a sling and give me a thirty-day leave so I could recuperate with my family in Birmingham. Other patients in the hospital laughed when they heard my request, but the doctor agreed; the patient with bad blood was going home.

That was the beginning of the end of my World War II military service. After my leave, the doctors decided that my arm had improved and the operation was not needed. Then with much hesitation, a doctor told me, "We don't know how to deal with the blood situation. You'll have to be careful as it will lead to serious health issues. We're recommending an honorable discharge as further duty will not be possible."

Beginning at Oak Ridge, Tennessee, and ending at Bikini Atoll, I had participated in the Manhattan Project, which built the atomic bomb, and I ended with a test of the weapon in Project Crossroads. The personal journey had come full circle.

The atomic bomb had been life-changing. Few of the informed discuss publicly what it did or what it can do. It brought death and devastation to those who wanted to conquer the world. One is reminded of the ruling kings recorded in the book of Chronicles and book of Kings in our Bible. Death and destruction came to the multitudes of the kings due to their desire to conquer their neighbors. Human nature never changes.

While this is not a chosen way for believers in the Lord Jesus Christ, it is memorable for two reasons. God permits humanity to have a nature foreign to His godly plan, to sin by devising methods of death and destruction; He requires the participants to suffer the consequences. It is intriguing how God uses ungodly activity for His purposes. This is shown in the glaring evidence of the crucifixion of our Lord Jesus Christ.

There is a second and most important unintended consequence for humanity. The terribly destructive bomb has now become the greatest deterrent to world war humanity has ever known. Major powers have it, but to use it would mean destruction to a degree never seen before. The human loss of the first explosion was much less than what a future nuclear explosion would cause. It is this ultimate destructive weapon possessed by adversaries that now holds back the ungodly who want to become the new Hitlers.

Today, millions are dying by other methods used to maintain control. The threat of massive destruction deters these killers only momentarily; it will not stop sinning humankind.

God's providential plan for His faithful is in place. We are living during a time when humanity stands on the brink. God is poised to make a final move with Christ's return. Evil will be eliminated. The faithful will be delivered.

This is the plan revealed in God's Word. It is not humanity that is sacred; it is people's souls made in God's image that will be preserved. Jesus entered our world to put the final piece in place. It is our call. Under the blood of Jesus, we will be those left standing in the jargon of combat.

There will be a final moment when evil is banished with a power far greater than humanity has devised. The urge to destroy will yield to the power of redeeming love for all eternity. This plan was sealed and certified at the cross. We must take up the cross in the name and power of our Lord.

CHAPTER 8

The Call of God

For when I preach the gospel I cannot boast, I am
compelled to preach. (1 Corinthians 9:16)

Time at home is always refreshing for those in the military.
Certain things had been neglected or changed while I was
away. Being on a timed furlough made the days pass quickly
for me. I returned to the hospital, and the diagnosis was the same.
The doctors agreed on an honorable discharge with orders to visit a
VA hospital if further treatment was necessary. That ended more than
three years in the military for me, someone whose real life was about
to begin.

The psalmist wrote about the providence of God, "The Lord will
watch over our coming and going both now and forevermore" (Psalm
121:8). Here is divine watchcare. Mary Edna's father, who owned a
service station, spent much of his daily life at West End Baptist Church
as a deacon, a leader of the community, and the director of a very large
Sunday school.

The godly influence of Arthur and Madge Burke, Mary Edna's
father and mother, was a factor in all the following. For them, attending
church, working in the church, and singing in the choir were events

as natural as eating with the Burke family of two adults, one girl, and two boys. Those activities were evidence of their personal beliefs and relationship with God.

The Burke family home was the haven God used to care for my wife and our baby when I was in the military. They were instruments God used to shape the life of someone who was to serve God in answer to His call for the rest of his life.

A large group of young adults met at the church each Sunday evening. Programs for group study were distributed, and volunteers spoke to the group and shared material that focused on Christian responsibilities and lifestyles for growing Christians.

Having been with a bunch of soldiers—sometimes marching, sometimes flying, always mouthing with one another—I never found communicating with others to be a problem. The program parts of the study were informative but easy. I had avoided volunteering in the military for three years, but I readily agreed to speak at our church meetings; it was the thing God wanted.

Giving those programs to a large group was the training I needed for my days ahead. It was also a lesson in how the Holy Spirit leads those who serve. Sharing God's Word made me more aware that to be effective, I needed God's power.

Going to church was keeping the Lord's day holy for me, and that was a great asset considering how most of the world observed the day. For the young Green family, church attendance became as normal as breathing.

As do larger churches, West End Baptist had a place for everyone including our baby, Jackie Lee. My wife and I could go to Bible study and never think for a moment about the care and safety of our child.

To unbelievers, the following is without merit or not understood. To believers, the following is a message from God through His Spirit concerning conversion in salvation. God's messages to believers relates to their daily lives, needs, and conduct as Christians as well as the work they are to do in the kingdom. A personal message of enlistment by

God's Spirit to an individual for work in His kingdom is described here as a call from God.

To clarify this and what follows, here are the words of Jesus Christ concerning the Holy Spirit in the life of redeemed souls as recorded in John 14:10–15.

> If you love me, keep my commands. And I will ask the Father and he will give you another advocate to help you and be with you forever—the Spirit of truth. The world cannot accept him, because it neither sees him nor knows him. But you know him, for he lives with you and will be in you. I will not leave you as orphans; I will come to you. Before long, the world will not see me anymore, but you will see me. Because I live, you also will live. On that day you will realize that I am in my Father, and you are in me, and I am in you.

The Sunday morning that changed my life began as usual. I was sitting on the back row with the usual group when Pastor Smith's message came with an inspired spirit loud and clear. He was from the old ministerial school. When he reached his final point, he would close the huge pulpit Bible as a signal that the end of worship was near. After that, the altar was open for those making public decisions concerning their salvation, Christian service, personal life decisions, or to have a moment of prayer with the pastor. It was a time to sing, praise God, and respond as His Spirit led them. Professing Christians were overjoyed to see worshipers making decisions.

Then it came. A message as clear as daylight. The Holy Spirit spoke: *Jack, I want you to spend your life preaching for Me.* It was such a vivid, pointed, and personal message. I looked around to see if some young friend had spoken those words. When I saw that no one was looking in my direction, I thought, *This was a message from God!*

God's call to vocational kingdom service comes in many ways. It is always personal and heard only by the called until the called share it.

It is so personal that few studies can explain it. Any such call that can be defined in human terms is a counterfeit. It is personal, meant only for the one intended to receive it from a God of love. When received, it can be refused, but it can never be forgotten.

The morning worship ended. Most Sundays, we stood around with other young people talking about our evening plans. On that day, I whispered to Mary Edna, "Get the baby. We're going home. There's something you must know." After several puzzling moments and some hesitation, she went for the baby. We left to go to our rented house several miles away.

On the way home, Mary did not say anything about our leaving the church so quickly before we said our goodbyes though I was sure she wondered about that. In later years, she received quiet respect in those personal moments. They helped avoid strong and opposing discussions.

The silence ended when we reached home. The questions came pouring out. "What happened? Why did we leave the church so suddenly?"

"Mary Edna, sitting in church this morning during the invitation for decisions to be made public, God spoke to me. He said, 'Jack, I want you to spend your life preaching for me.'"

My tears were flowing at the thought of a wonderful, loving, heavenly Father speaking to one whose prayer life was juvenile and whose true obedience to Him was in the beginner's stage.

There were no tears in Mary Edna's eyes, but I saw that she was troubled. It almost floored me when she said, "Jack, I didn't marry a preacher!" Her statement startled me. We were both crying. We agreed to pray. On our knees, we had a clear and pointed talk with the Father. We needed help. We needed assurance.

It came to my mind that what Mary Edna said about not having wanted to marry a preacher had been framed by church trouble involving a preacher in whom she had placed her confidence. Remembering that took the edge off her answer for me, but it did not solve a problem.

My understanding concerning personal surrender by a life partner came later in life. If I had had that understanding earlier, I would have understood my wife's response. The surrender of a husband or wife for special service is individual. Unity is a matter for God to address. It requires patience and trust to see it happen.

At church that evening the invitation given was exactly like those at the close of morning worship. It was time for me to respond to God. While walking down the aisle to take the hand of the pastor, I had but one thought: *This is surrender to God's call for the rest of my life.* No other had heard God call me to preach His gospel; it was personal. God's messages to individuals for specific purposes are sacred communication.

Others may act in good conscience with a different response. For me, after much prayer, an immediate response has always taken away delay and given me an opening for God's call to bless. It has resulted in a life that has brought me total satisfaction as to answering and fulfilling God's directions for service in His kingdom. His blessings yet abound!

I told Pastor Smith about God's call to me during the morning worship to preach His Word, to serve Him the rest of my life. The pastor shared this with the church. There was a hush, but that was followed by an overwhelming response of hugs, handshakes, congratulations, and many questions. Mary Edna quietly slipped out to get the baby.

The day closed with a question mark. If God gives you a clear and undisputed call for ministry that you make public in the church but your wife says she is not in step with that call, what do you do? I could not answer that question; I had never been in that situation before. I wondered how I would answer God. In any event, I had made God's message to me public.

It was not too long before the answer came. God taught how His angels work. His providence became as clear as the morning sun. When Mary Edna told her father about her feelings concerning my call to ministry, he surprisingly said, "I have an opening here at the shop. Jack will fill it nicely. I'll expect him in the morning." It was as if Papa Burke had not heard what she had said about God's call to me and her thoughts about that. But he was concerned about us and our need for an income. He supplied the answer. As are many of God's providential acts, it was unexpected but timely. Arthur Burke was an angel in the providence of God for one who would fulfill His call.

Taking the job meant that I could not immediately start studying for the ministry and gain a good theological education, and I knew Mary Edna had to be willing to support my call. The signal was clear. I would not answer God's call until all were on board. The faith response has opened the way. In God's time, His plan will be fulfilled.

CHAPTER 9

In God's Time

The Lord has done great things for us, and we are filled with joy. (Psalm 126:3)

The work at the service station was rewarding particularly after my years in the military filled with roll calls, daily regimens, and taps; it refreshed my spirit. My call to a preaching ministry was put on the back burner—no mention of it for weeks. My work at the gas station was calming and gave me time to think. We had daily Bible reading and prayer but no discussion of my preparation for ministry.

The conclusion was simple. If God's call was real and undeniably sacred, it was not something to treat as an arguing point but as a goal. If the call was genuine, God would see it done. There would be no manipulating or conversations about the present situation. There was no one with a victim mentality in our home.

In the summer of my first year home from military service, Mr. Burke asked us if we would like to accompany him to Ridgecrest, North Carolina in July, for the Sunday school week of training and inspiration. After my mother-in-law agreed to babysit Jackie, we accepted the invitation. We were thrilled. This would be our real honeymoon!

The retreat center that summer was crowded by those from many

Baptist churches. The classes were informative and well organized. In the evening, there was a worship time for all participants in an auditorium that seated a thousand. The speaker was the president of the Southern Baptist Sunday School Board.

The preacher for the night was a stranger, but it seemed God was leading me to talk to and pray with him about our future.

After being seated for the service, the desire to speak to the preacher was overwhelming. Being excused, I went behind the auditorium. Seeing a choir member I inquired as to where the preacher could be found. He told me. Moving through the milling choir members, the preacher was found sitting with his bible in his lap.

I begged his pardon for interrupting him and said, "Sir, I need a prayer partner. Several weeks ago, God called me into ministry. My wife said she had not married a preacher. Would you spend a few minutes in prayer with me about this as we are waiting for service to begin?"

"Why sure," was his easy answer. He slipped out of his chair and fell on his knees in an attitude of prayer after asking my name. The next few minutes were a blur. We were praying as people were stepping all around us to get into the choir. After thanking him for his time and apologizing for interrupting his preparation time, I rejoined our family.

There is always a challenge to prayer as to time, place, subject, and personal demeanor. Godly faith assures there will be an answer as Jesus promised, but it will happen in His time. All or none of that may have been present while we were on our knees. The one great memory I have was how quiet my heart had become about the entire matter.

I returned to the auditorium seat; there were no questions. The music was more beautiful than ever. Little memory of the sermon lingers, but the result is etched on my soul.

When concluding his message, the board president paused for a moment as if wrestling with something mental or spiritual. He began to close the worship. Abruptly stopping, he said, "I do not normally do this, but there is something we need to think about. If there are some here to whom God is speaking about their life, their future, or some problem, I want them to come here. Let me pray with you about it."

There were over a thousand people in the auditorium, but there was just one on my heart as I prayed through the remarks of the speaker. After singing one stanza of the hymn, Mary Edna looked at me and asked, "Do you want to walk with me, or do you want me to walk alone?"

It was clear. God had spoken to the problem she had been dealing with for more than six months! I said, "Go ahead. I'll be right behind you." Praises were leaping from my spirit as we ended the walk hand in hand. The preacher had become God's angel!

The talk with the speaker was brief. All three of us bowed. Mary Edna's was a prayer of total surrender. Mine was a prayer of praise for a God who answers prayers in His time for our good and His kingdom.

We floated back to our seats. It was the night when we could look back and say, "The Lord has done great things."

The trip home was like time away from every soul in the universe. We rejoiced in God's glory and blessings while making tentative plans. By God's providential plan and love, we became one in mind, heart, and spirit.

CHAPTER 10

Expect the Unexpected

Trust in God's Unfailing Love. (Psalm 52:8)

As we started planning our future, a startling, unexpected family event occurred. I had been thinking about enrolling in Howard College, a Baptist school in the eastern part of Birmingham. Tuition would be free for a would-be minister of the gospel, but not having a car made my plans to attend that school a little difficult.

It was almost imperative for us to move closer to the school. Someone else who worked at the gas station said he had an apartment in the back of his house we could rent. It was a three-room apartment with bath near the West End Baptist Hospital. The rear entrance to the hospital was near and faced the apartment. This was God's providence as we shall see!

Our daughter, Jackie Lee, had been somewhat premature. As a baby, she had stomach pain from time to time. No one thought much of it, and we treated her spells of pain as mild cholic.

But in the early hours before dawn one day, she awoke screaming in pain. I carried her to the emergency room, which was just a few hundred feet from our back door.

The emergency room doctor said surgery might be necessary for our baby girl. Dr. Lovell had been trained in surgery at Duke University but had chosen to be a family doctor in West End. As he was our family doctor, we asked for him to be called if surgery for Jackie Lee was required.

God was about to demonstrate how He used angels to do His work. It was a lesson I will never forget.

Dr. Lovell examined her and told us that she had been born with two sections of her lower bowel very unstable. Two adjoining pieces of the bowel had telescoped and locked! He called it intussusception, and he said it was an illness primarily in children. We knew it had been with her since birth three years earlier. He said it would require immediate surgery.

It was time to pray with other family members who had joined us. Several hours passed. We thought there was a complication with surgery as it was taking so long.

In the sixth hour, Dr. Lovell came from surgery. His green clothes were soaking wet. He looked completely drained. But there was something of a sparkle in his eyes. He said that the affected tissue in the bowel was seriously deteriorated and that he had considered replacing it with sheep's intestines. He paused to speak of his mental pain about replacing a piece of bowel in a baby so young. He said, "A three-year-old should never have to live the rest of her life with the replacement of a section of intestines."

With that lingering feeling of remorse for our baby, Dr. Lovell said, "It came to my mind that maybe a heated compress could be applied for a length of time to see if it changed the physical condition of the bruised intestine before having to remove it." He said, however that was not the recommended procedure for a locked bowel in a child.

The doctor made a startling statement. "After talking with God, I decided to use hot compresses on the affected area. The first compress changed the appearance of the intestine. In fact, there was a small change with each compress." He had tears in his eyes when he said, "I was witnessing a miracle!"

After four hours of applications, there was success! The intestine that had been blocked with no blood flow was then functioning! The doctor spoke of the evident jubilation in surgery. He said, "I sat down and thanked God before closing the stomach."

When he related this to two very young parents with family and friends who had joined us, all were in tears. Hearing a doctor say he had seen a miracle and had sat and prayed to thank God was a thrill to the soul. None of us had ever heard this kind of talk from a professional such as Dr. Lovell. He was God's angel for Jackie Lee and us.

Jackie went through a long period of recovery. Penicillin was a new drug on the market then, and the doctor prescribed it for her to protect against infection. He said the area was vulnerable to complications caused by the surgery; he wanted to see her twice a day to check on the healing.

We were standing by Jackie's bed on the eighth day, and we were concerned. She could not focus her eyes. Rather than squirm and chatter as she had been doing, she was not moving. It was as if she was comatose. Mary Edna and I noticed the condition at the same time. We knew something had taken place during the night and wondered if she was relapsing.

When Dr. Lovell came in, we asked him to look at Jackie's eyes, which she could not focus. It was as if she were blind. Dr. Lovell looked somewhat stunned after examining her surgery wound, eyes, heart, and blood pressure. His response was immediate. She was suffering some side effects of the penicillin, and he immediately took her off the drug.

The change was almost immediate. After twenty-four hours, Jackie began acting like a baby again. Her body was healing. It was as if she knew something great had been taking place. There were no more pains. Our prayers were being answered!

During this experience, as young parents, as young believers about to launch a life of service to our loving, heavenly Father, we realized we were on a learning curve. Here is a small part of what we learned.

Christians are not assured pain-free lives, but life is different for believers who trust Jesus Christ in faith. Expecting the unexpected is a lifestyle. There is a negative influence on the circumstances of life by a destructive force of evil in this world that believers experience daily in body and spirit as a result of a bad decision made in the Garden of Eden.

These expectations of life were thoroughly prepared for by a loving Father. God built a remarkable body structure. Take any element of humanity, body or spirit. Explain how it came to be and how it should be treated so there will never be a time of unexpected pain in body or soul. It is not possible. Causes may or may not be identified. Humanity believes there are answers in the human scheme of things. Medical science is so successful that many swear by it as the ultimate path to humanity's existence. That is a failed belief.

The same for the spiritual aspects of life. While some scorn or neglect the Bible, believers know it provides answers to the questions of the human pilgrimage that defy the logic of the smartest unbelieving scholar.

God can make a human in nine months! It is a given that is seldom mentioned when dealing with daily unexpected body and health issues. It would seem logical to turn to the One who made it to ask questions about healing it. That was done in our experience. It works!

We get our answers in our hearts, not our minds. The head tells the heart that there is something out there that can give us stability while we are dealing with the unexpected. The God of miracles is there for those who believe that the One who made the body will care for it if it is turned over to Him in faith! It is the human soul that God takes across the threshold of death to eternity.

This is how believers live as they experience the unexpected. Life is met with a faith in the Lord Jesus that makes a loving God alive and leading in any circumstances. The Holy Spirit leads as we expect the unexpected to be a means for God to reveal His love. God provides for a believer.. Notice the first seven letters in Providence is PROVIDE.

CHAPTER 11

The Launchpad

My help comes from the Lord. (Psalm 121:2)

T he grace of God provided a shelter for three who needed a place to get it all together after a tremendous scare. Jackie was recovering. The Burke family was the foundational stone God put in place for us. Madge Burke, a loving mother-in-law, was like another mother to Jackie. Their house became our house as work at the station was nearing an end. Finances were tight.

There was another addition to the family. God gave us a son! Arthur Douglas was born while the family was in a state of transition. School was not a choice but a necessity. It was to be the launchpad for a ministry that would glorify the Lord and bless the glorifiers. How and when were decisions we had to make.

All ministers of the gospel are schooled someplace and somehow to prepare them to share God's Word, and I was no exception. Howard College, the forerunner of the present Samford University, was a convenience that proved to be a blessing as it provided me the education I needed for a God-blessed ministry.

College opened the door for me, someone who knew little or nothing about the Bible. It was not only a choice but a necessity! The

Alabama Baptist Convention had provided for ministerial students to not have to pay much if any tuition. The Veterans Administration had been authorized to provide low-rent residences for those who had served in World War II, and we got an apartment near downtown Birmingham for just $50 a month, which we paid for with the disability money I had received for my shoulder injury. God had provided for tuition and housing! No one had to remind us who was in control, who was paving the way for the future.

With new housing a reality, school became the center of our attention. It was a shock to learn there were more than two hundred students enrolled in Howard College in preparation for ministry.

Military service had given me adequate preparation for college; former soldiers could manage their time and requirements with ease. While some younger students were struggling, we were rejoicing. Learning how to lead in a secular setting was a blessing! In all aspects of the need for the days ahead, from Bible study to human relations in life among believers, these were days of preparation.

The school offered two avenues to a bachelor's degree. One lasted three rather than four years, but it required taking classes in the summer. Taking the shorter course seemed best for me.

Shortly after I enrolled, the professor who was sponsoring the freshmen class learned of my military service and asked me if he could give my name to the officer nominating group, and I said yes. The freshmen voted me in as their class president. This was the first of several events that shaped me for leadership as a preacher.

The Reverend James Butler, pastor of the West End Baptist Church, had given me the opportunity to preach on two occasions, but that was the extent of my preaching experience then. Howard College had a student-led week of worship that focused on God's guidance for life. Being a leader of the freshmen made my name known to those selecting preachers for the week. It was an honor for me to be chosen as one of the five student preachers.

Preaching the first sermon to a packed auditorium of students and professors was a challenge for me. When one of the preacher students became ill, I was asked to give the closing message. That was God's way of placing a young, untrained student in a place where he could develop his preaching skills for the years ahead.

Many opportunities for service opened for me through my preaching. Major (addressed by the rank he held in World War I) Harwell Davis, the president of Howard College, came to give me personal praise for my effort, a great honor. He and I became close friends.

Some of the fraternities were engaged in activities that concerned the president. He asked me to talk to their leaders one by one to point out his concerns. I had been asked to assist the yearbook editor by arranging for pictures to be taken of each fraternity and sorority, so I could accomplish both tasks with those individual visits. We got the yearbook pictures, and I gave the president a favorable report of cooperation by the fraternities.

The college had dropped football during the war, so a group of former military men got together to bring football back to the college. They formed a club and asked if I would lead the effort. It meant raising money, recruiting players, scheduling games, providing insurance and transportation, and finding volunteer coaches. That was quite a challenge for a sophomore preparing for the ministry, but with the help of willing, military-trained men, it fell into place. Major Davis gave his approval to use the athletic field, and the leaders of athletics in the faculty agreed to help.

As the former president of the freshmen and then a senator representing the sophomore class, I had an opening to ask the student government to contribute from the student funds received for the annual yearbook. Half of those funds were given to the group, which was named The Sportsmen Club. Students helped the athletic director build bleachers for the games on Howard's athletic field. For their support and work, the students would be admitted free to the games.

Raising money to put a team on the field in a few months gave me an opportunity to meet merchants and friends, and the support they gave was amazing. There was enthusiasm and excitement about returning football to Howard College. In one of the last games they had played before the war cancelled the program, Howard had tied the University of Alabama, so visions of great things were abounding for the future.

Some were ready to bank on that future. A major sporting goods company loaned the club football gear worth $5,000. When told it might not get its money, the reply was, "We are looking toward the future. If you cannot pay, there will be better days ahead for Howard to have a football team!"

The season went well. There were many challenging and wonderful experiences that demanded leadership. They were times when God gave the team members a chance to learn the meaning of honesty and integrity.

After we played a game in Selma, the money promised from gate receipts seemed short. One of the student managers was asked to count the people watching the game. The bus driver returning the team to the college was asked to stop at the stadium gate; some players opened the gate and the ticket booth, and the team sat under a field light and counted the tickets.

The team leaders went to a café where the after-game meal was underway and confronted the manager of the opposing team. After a short conversation, the team returned with several hundred dollars more than the team had received.

There were times when God's care of His children was evident. On one memorable occasion, a player who was a pilot in the Air National Guard checked out a plane and flew the team for a game in North Carolina!

On the return trip on a Sunday morning, the weather had closed the Birmingham airport. The pilot was refused landing instructions and told by the control tower operator to take the flight to Montgomery. It was eight in the morning, and Montgomery was a hundred miles south. I was in the copilot seat and heard that order. I told the pilot that I had an obligation to preach at eleven o'clock sixty-five miles from Birmingham.

The pilot told the tower there was not enough fuel to make it to Montgomery as his takeoff field had not refueled him. He told us, "Hold on. We're going to land right here in Birmingham." When the nose of the plane cleared the outer fence of the landing strip, it seemed I could reach out and touch it. Service at the church began on time with me, the preacher, present.

After the team played eight games, its members wanted to do something about football in the future for the college. The $5,000 was our only outstanding debt. The Sportsmen Club asked Major Davis if it would be possible for the club president to speak to the trustees regarding football in the future, and he agreed.

At that meeting, we presented to the trustees our idea of a college-sponsored football team and our need for $7,000 to do that. Major Davis, who knew of the $5,000 the team owed, asked about the extra $2,000. We told him about how much support the student body had shown the team and that the extra money was for a campus-wide party to thank them that we wanted to hold in the gym, and he agreed to that.

The trustees voted to sponsor a team but without scholarships for the players, but a year later, they agreed to partial work scholarships for selected team members. It is notable that Bobby Bowden, one of the players who later coached at Howard and became exceedingly successful at Florida State, received the first work scholarship. A full scholarship program is now in place at Samford, a continuation of the early beginnings at Howard.

In the early days, it was evident to Major Davis that something big had taken place. He looked to the future. Howard College did not have an alumni office. The key to the planning for a new campus would involve the help of graduates, many of whom were ministers, and others who were very successful in their professional and business pursuits. Howard College had prepared them for their success.

Major Davis asked this future minister to be the first Howard College alumni secretary. The trustees knew of my work with the Sportsmen Club, and they agreed to appoint me to that position. I started my work in an office in the gymnasium complex, and I had a secretary to help me. Major Harwell Davis turned out to be God's angel in fashioning the leadership skills of this young preacher. It was a strange but a God-blessed venture. At that time, I was a senior with a family and a part-time minister at a church.

Alumni clubs were organized for those in several professions, and I received support of alumni in several cities. They became active in aiding Samford University, today a premier educational institution for the Lord.

Graduation in 1950 ended an active college career. I had served in the student senate for three years, and as vice president my senior year. I had the honor of being chosen as the school's Outstanding Student; the John R. Mott award accented what God was doing in a life dedicated to His service. God has a plan for every life.

As for learning leadership, I was humbled to receive an invitation to Omicron Delta Kappa honorary leadership fraternity. The honors came because God had blessed me with a dedicated wife and a home where I could study. My grades entitled me to membership in the Phi Beta Kappa honorary fraternity.

Everything I accomplished at college came by the grace of God; His plan was for His glory. Mary Edna took some college classes, but she supported and loved me in an unmatched way when school, staff work, and pastoring were demanding my time. God's plan was to thoroughly prepare me for the ministry that lay ahead for me. His providential plan revealed to me how He fashions the lives of His servants.

After graduation from Howard College, I entered full-time ministry in a church and later as a missionary abroad. This will be shared with you as the work of God's angels. It is the record of a loving God whose plan was followed and the times when He used angels on my behalf. Through it all, my wife and I were singing, "Praise God from whom all blessings flow!"

Chapter 12

The Way Forward

Faith sees the invisible, believes the incredible, and
receives the impossible.

—Adrian Rogers

This quote is from the website LOVEWORTHFINDING. Adrian
Rogers and I served in the same Baptist church grouping in
Florida. He was a wonderful pastor and friend who spoke
many times in our church, and that was always a blessing. The devotion
from which this quotation came included a statement that is our strong
belief: "Doubt sees the obstacles; faith sees the way."

All pastors have some remarkable experiences that defy logic
including how they became pastors of this or that church. I have
experienced what many would call miracles, but they were the
providence of God in action; thinking about them in that way makes
them logical. Labeling God's angelic care as a miracle is another way
of identifying the unexplainable work of our loving heavenly Father
for His children. It is most evident in the work of pastoral ministers.

There is a protocol for the process of pastoral calls to churches; it is
a coordinated action between the body of Christ and a minister of the
gospel under God's mandate for service. If it is truly of God, His Holy

Spirit will bring church and minister to a covenant. This is a call by a church for service and a ministerial acceptance to serve that church.

It should be remembered that actions in the service of God are always subject to human error. God permits it as we shall see in the following record.

Every saved soul, not just those called to ministry, should have an active faith. Jesus said, "Produce fruit in keeping with repentance," and He warned, "The ax is already at the root of the trees, and every tree that does not produce good fruit will be cut down and thrown into the fire" (Matthew 3:8, 10). This is basic to salvation for all. God expects a high level of faith, obedience, and loyalty from those who accept His call for special kingdom service. When one accepts the call of God for such service but fails to continue it, that is a judgment by God, not by humankind. By the same measure, one who continues for a lifetime in such service expresses a love in daily care that defies human understanding.

My ministerial journey revealed the work of God's angels and His providence in my pastoral service to five stateside churches and one in another country. God's providential work is recorded here.

Ohatchee Baptist Church

In the beginning … (Genesis 1:1)

Because I lived several miles from Howard College and did not have a car, I had to hitchhike there every day. One day, I was dropped off several blocks from college and had to walk to the campus.. William Weaver, the student campus pastor, was leaving the campus that morning as I was arriving. After our mutual greetings, he asked me a shocking question: "Jack, where are you preaching Sunday?" "I'm not preaching," I told him. He asked if I would like to preach the coming Sunday at the Ohatchee Baptist Church, and he told me how far it was from Birmingham.

I told him I lacked transportation, and he said, "The train goes right through Ohatchee. You can take it and get there about nine in the morning. It returns about nine in the evening." That sealed the deal. We lived just across the street from the Birmingham Terminal Station. That request for service launched my preaching ministry. After that Sunday service, I was asked to return, and I did—for over two years. William Weaver's request for service launched my preaching ministry; he was an angel God sent to launch my ministry.

That preaching experience prepared me for the future.. On one occasion, an itinerant preacher came to have a community revival complete with a tent in a field to accommodate worshipers. The news of the revival and the plans being made caused much concern because the preacher did not have a good reputation; he did not seem to want or need cooperation from local pastors when planning his work.

After considering the progress that preacher was making for the revival, I decided to discuss the matter with the church deacons, two of whom were mail carriers and the third a farmer. It was more convenient for me to talk to the mailmen about my concerns, and I did. The two listened quietly, and the possibility of publicly disrupting the preacher's plans with a pastoral church announcement was suggested.

When Deacon Goode said, "Brother Green," I knew it was time to listen to this Sunday school teacher, Bible scholar, and praying man. He continued. "We need to talk further. If we are not careful, we will violate one of the principles revealed by a godly teacher in the Bible." He spoke of how Peter and the apostles were about to be killed. He said a Jewish teacher went against his own people when he told them that if they killed these Christians, they might well be going against God. Brother Poole suggested that I be given the bible reference. "Tell the pastor where this is found so he can read it for himself. " Brother Goode said it could be found in the fifth chapter of the book of Acts. The teacher's name was Gamaliel."

The meeting ended. It was time for another decision. It was made after praying in a quiet place. The scripture read exactly as Deacon Goode had cited it. That necessitated my meeting with the preacher who had brought about the decision and discussion, but my discussion with the deacons and study of the scripture had given me a new mind about the situation.

I spoke to the preacher, and his response was cool. When he told me about the dates he had planned for his revival, I told him they were the same dates of the Ohatchee Baptist revival. He said, "Well, Brother Green, we can change our dates. How about the week following your revival?" I said, "Why don't the three of you join us for our revival? You can announce your plans to our congregation."

The preacher smiled and agreed to that. I left with deep satisfaction, a feeling that the Lord would be pleased with how this had been handled. And I was thankful for Brother Goode's suggestion.

On the first night of the revival, the preacher and his sons were sitting in the front row. During the announcement period, they were recognized; the preacher spoke about his plans and invited all present to attend his revival.

The following is not a reflection on any person or his or her work; it was an event that told us how God handled problems or events when we took our hands off and trusted His control.

Twenty-three souls became Christians and made their open confession at the close of each evening of worship at our revival. One was a twenty-six-year-old man who had a reputation for evil in the community.

On the night following his conversion, he asked permission to give another testimony at the close of worship. The itinerant preacher and family were present when this man told the church how he had rejoiced after becoming a Christian: "I was so carried away that I didn't pay attention to where I was walking. The town had dug a hole about eight feet deep near the side of the street for some repairs. I did not see it in the dark and fell into it. There was no one near. I prayed and asked God to send help. A black man walking home heard my cry and began running in fright, but I finally got through to him. He came back and gave me his hand, and I got out of the hole. It was God answering my prayer." We rejoiced with the new convert. It became clear that all of us had heard a rejoicing testimony.

When our meeting was concluded, the community seemed to feel the new group that was having meetings should be supported. The crowds filled the tent for the first nights. At the close of the first week, the pastor gave his interpretation of the young man's testimony he had heard at the Ohatchee Baptist revival. He left an impression of mockery about the young man's conversion; he likened him to some drunk falling into a hole. That had been the previous lifestyle of the new convert, which the preacher did not know.

The result of the preacher's interpretation became quickly evident. The property on which the tent stood belonged to an uncle of the new convert who had given his testimony. Before the preacher finished his remarks, the switch for the tent lights that was in the uncle's house was turned off, and the tent became as dark as the night surrounding it.

As the people were leaving, someone dropped a lit cigarette. The straw on the ground had been there for more than two weeks. The fire began to blaze. Before it could be extinguished, the tent and all the equipment were destroyed. When this news was received, there was a sad feeling as to the result of the preacher's meeting. The tent should not have been destroyed.

That was a lesson for life. The first impression may have been accurate as to the purpose of the preacher. However, the conclusion of his meeting had not pleased God. Negative or derogatory comments even innocently made by a preacher in jest are acts of ungodliness.

There are times when God's work must be left to God. His providential care can be trusted. I avoided making a tremendous mistake in the treatment of a fellow minister because a godly deacon knew biblical scripture. Brother Goode became God's angel at work!

Interlude

Do not be like the horse or mule, which have no understanding. (Psalm 32:9)

My book is not about perfect Christians, and the following will prove that. The scripture I use here might describe my thinking better. While I was pastoring the church at Ohatchee, God's Spirit brought a miracle. No one had been baptized by the church in several years. In a revival, God saved a host of souls, who were baptized in a creek. Each Sunday, the church was filled. God blessed the church and the town of Ohatchee.

Billy Green, my brother, a master sergeant in the 167th Regiment, 31st Infantry Division of the National Guard, told me that his unit needed a chaplain. Having served in World War II, I would have an automatic officer commission in the National Guard if I accepted the position. My brother's request did not seem to me to require much thought or prayer, which was a critical mistake. All requests for time and service for a full-time servant of God should be a time for prayer.

I thought that service in the National Guard would not interfere with my Ohatchee ministry. Also, Billy had seldom if ever asked me for help. He was not a practicing Christian at the time, so he would not have thought about talking with God about his request. I did not lay my brother's request before our Lord which was the right thing to do.

When I signed up, I was promised I would not have to serve on Sundays. For a couple of months, there were no problems. Graduation from college had given more time to spend in Ohatchee, and God had provided an old car for transportation to the church for services every Sunday instead of every other Sunday, as was the need when I became pastor..

Then came a bombshell. President Truman ordered the 31st Infantry Division to active service. This was Korean war. Hearing that order made me realize that I had not laid my enlistment before our loving Father; He had not vetted my personal decision.

My ministry at Ohatchee ended just a couple of months after the church had gone full time. God didn't plan the abrupt ending, but he permitted it. When His plan is different from ours, that can result in disobedience. Obedience comes after prayer has brought what is believed to be God's will for the moment.

God's providence was evident to me in the months that followed, but the joy of being in His perfect will was not. It was an interlude for which there had been no planning and very little satisfaction. The desire for daily obedience remained, but my circumstances were quite different from those of a pastor.

This is a caution to believers who rejoice in free will, which makes salvation a personal decision. The redeemed who serve God must get His permission for life-changing decisions to be in accordance with His will. This can be determined only by prayer and fulfilled by obedience.

For salvation and in daily decisions, obedience to the leadership of the Holy Spirit, the resident voice of God in believers, is a must. Conviction of sin comes through the Spirit. Prayer of forgiveness is the satisfaction God gives through His Spirit. Our daily decisions get a yes-or-no impulse from God in our spirits. Christians come to know this as God's leadership.

As concerns military service, I was blessed to serve others and do the Lord's work, but the fulfillment I received when in our Father's perfect will was not present. That was the only time in my years of ministry when the Spirit of God withheld His confirmation in the heart for service in His kingdom.

My service was an interlude in my church ministry, but the time spent in that endeavor for our country was not degrading or an insult to God's work in an individual. There was never a day when my personal devotion to our Lord was interrupted. It became clear that God blessed my time serving our country. There was evidence that those who came under my influence were blessed. It was an interlude for me, not for God, who cared for and guided me. Kingdom service in an unplanned interlude is not exempt from God's blessing.

It was a busy interlude from my church ministry. The war in Korea had taken a high toll on officers, who were needed to train combat soldiers. The commanding colonel asked me if I could take on duties other than those of a chaplain.

I had been a tail gunner in World War II and had served as a barracks chief. Those "other duties" the colonel asked me to do included being a security platoon leader; managing a baseball team; being a mess officer and leading a troop caravan from North Carolina to Texas for field training.

There was an opportunity to preach to generals and privates. There was no opportunity to give an invitation or give disciple training. We were training men who were learning how to kill and dodge death rather than serve God and man in lives full of His presence and grace.

I learned a lesson about the need to seek God's will before satisfying mine. At age twenty-five, this young servant of the Lord learned a spiritual lesson in a ministry that would last until God makes the eternal call. It is indelibly written on his heart.

Linden Baptist Church

He is before all things, and in him all things hold together. (Colossians 1:17)

With the error of military service in mind, I thought it was time to talk with Major Davis, the president of Howard College. I had served on his staff during my senior year there and had always found him to be down to earth with the Lord as his guide. I did not mention to him that I thought my service in the military had been a mistake; we talked as as two friends who always enjoyed each other. He was deeply interested in what I had experienced, and we did some catching up. Remembering the good times of things God has provided is always a boost to the human spirit.

As we were finishing our visit, the major posed a question: "Jack, where are you preaching this Sunday?" I told him that as my military service had just ended, I had no preaching appointments on my calendar. He asked, "Would you like to preach?" This was like asking a baby if he liked milk. My reply was short, quick, and openly positive: "Yes sir!"

Major told me of his childhood in Marengo County. "The folks down that way have never forgotten me. The Baptist church in Linden called to ask if I would preach this Sunday. I accepted the appointment before checking my calendar. I had an earlier obligation that I do not want to ignore. If you would be kind enough to handle this, I'll give you the contact names and inform them of my decision to have you take this Sunday for me." God used Major Harwell Davis, president of Howard College, as an angel!

There was a great lesson here. Our heavenly Father knew of my heart being heavy for ignoring Him when enlisting in the National Guard. The invitation came as an endorsement of a new phase of ministry. God holds things together for those He uses in His plan as servants in the world. Going before us, He had the new challenge already in His plan.

I had made plans during my last days of military service during the Korean war to attend Southern Seminary at Louisville, Kentucky, the place all my pastoral friends attended. It seemed to be the place God was leading me. I prayed about this and felt God wanted me to be a man of God in life and learning.

My time at Linden was pleasant. The people were friendly. The church had a pastor who seemed to be a caretaker, someone who paid attention to those present. He had done that for twelve years. The church was half full for worship. It accommodated two hundred at capacity.

Several days after my preaching engagement, I received a call from the chairman of the church's Pulpit Committee. He said his group wanted to talk to me. He asked me to give him a date for a return visit with the intent of discussing the future of the church and a call to become their pastor.

I told him about my plans for seminary, which seemed to be God's immediate imperative for me. He accepted that with a statement as to the unanimous vote of the committee regarding my call to Linden.

Several weeks passed during which I unwound from my military service. My children needed to be with me, and I needed to be with them. In retrospect, I see that it was a time when my family was forming. We did not know what the future held, but I had been accepted at the seminary, and I felt closer to God and my family than I had felt in the recent years.

One morning, the chairman of the Pulpit Committee at Linden Baptist Church asked me to come on Sunday, and I went. At the end of the worship service, the members of the congregation expressed their overwhelming appreciation for my message; they sincerely thanked me for my sermon and time.

Claude Perry, the chairman, who had become a friend, asked me to spend some time with his committee. That had not been the intent of his invitation to me to preach that Sunday, but somehow, there was a new presence when he gave the invitation. I felt that this was the movement of the Holy Spirit, that God was present that day.

At the pulpit committee meeting, several members spoke about the church's needs. The longer they spoke, the more I was convinced that something new had been added to the request. God was leading in a powerful way; I sensed that in their deep convictionas to my decision to be their pastor..

I asked myself, *Is this the place God will call me to and confirm as service to Him prior to my entering the seminary?* I needed more time to pray about that. God's leadership had changed the entire process. I told Brother Perry that I needed time to think about it, and he agreed.

Days morphed into a few enjoyable weeks I spent with my family, and I was asking God daily to lead as to my future. Brother Perry called again; he was ready for my answer, and he got it. God was sending me to a ministry that had not been in my plans which is often the way for a yielding servant. .

Over the next four years, God affirmed His call to me and His eternal blessings became evident. More than two hundred souls came to be God's children in new birth! God was in my decision to postpone attending seminary.

The joy of the Lord remains in my memory. He leads those who accept His plans and abandon the paths they are on, and they learn of His eternal providence as they trust and follow Him.

When I was serving in Korea, a former Linden member with whom I had a deep and lasting bond wrote to me sharing his need after he had lost his wife. That and many other ways, memories, and relationships confirm the providence of God when I followed His plan. Yes, God is before all things, and all things do hold together in Him!

Different Direction

> Send me your light and your faithful care, let them lead me. (Psalm 43:3)

God's faithful servants never know the direction God will send them as His plan unfolds and he reveals His providence. I faced a sharp and unexpected change during the end of my fourth year at Linden.

A young pastor could find no better place to serve than in that church in Marengo County. My wife was deep into a personal ministry of love and caring, and our two children were extremely satisfied. Then God laid out His plan.

A meeting of the Alabama Baptist Convention took place in Mobile. Most of my work in my local Baptist church was a result of my relationship with the convention. The convention featured speakers of interest to pastors.

One speaker was a pastor who had just returned from a visit to South Korea. He spoke about Korea's future. The war, which had recently ended, had been extremely painful. North Koreans wanted to establish communism throughout South Korea, which wanted to retain its semi-democrat form of government. The United States entered the war on behalf of South Korea. The conflict ended when President

Truman drew a line on a map of Korea dividing it into North and South Korea, as it remains today.

The Memphis pastor spoke about the need for missionaries to Korea. The Southern Baptist Convention relief programs were providing food and clothing the people of South Korea needed. He gave us a clear and challenging picture of missionary work.

I discussed this with another pastor from Marengo County after the presentation; we were both interested in the idea of missionary work in Korea. I retired for the night anticipating another long day at the convention, but sleep would not come. After a sleepless hour or so, I fell before the Lord in prayer to ask for peace, but it did not come. God spoke clearly about His call to missionary service. It needed verifying. After more prayer nothing changed. This had to be shared with Mary Edna.

Though it was two in the morning, I called Mary Edna, who was fearful when she heard my voice at that hour. She asked, "What's happened?" I assured her everything was fine to relieve her fears, but then I said, "God has called us to become foreign missionaries."

Her reply startled me: "I've known that for six months. You know, we always said that if God wanted to move a pastor, the pastor would get the message. Well, I've been waiting for God to move you."

In our home church prior to becoming a pastoral family, there were strong messages of missionary work and needs. As the leader of the Women Missionary Union in the Linden church and later for all the Baptist churches in Marengo country, Mary Edna had been greatly influenced by the concept of missionary work.

I returned from the conference and met with the leaders of the Linden church to announce my resignation. The response was overwhelming. Those who cared for our children in Bible classes and school were the most outspoken about their feelings, but they all honored the decision to prepare for missionary service.

My decision to postpone attending seminary four years earlier had been God's plan. Changing direction in a life of ministry requires the Lord's clear direction and guidance. I had been careful not to repeat my earlier mistake. Obeying the clear call to Linden had been a blessing. Ending it with a missionary call we could truly say, "This is of the Lord."

We received multiple expressions of appreciation and love as we prepared to leave Linden. The church was full for our final service with many standing outside. Some who had never shown concern gave us very kind remarks and expressed their regrets for our leaving.

The sheriff of Marengo country and his wife were great supporters of missions. He visited us one morning. Upon leaving he handed me a piece of paper. He said, "Pastor here is a list of clothing items from suits to shoes. We want you to go to the store and get all of them. Here's a signed check you can give to the merchant so he can fill out the total cost." He wished us well and promised to pray for us. It was time for a prayer of thanksgiving. This along with other actions of God's people strongly confirmed that our decision pleased God. Throughout our days of leaving, we were continuously shown other expressions of love. It has been said, "You cannot out-give God." We found that to be true.

There were other decisions of importance. When we stayed in Birmingham with family, I had to decide about seminary. I had previously settled on the seminary in Louisville, Kentucky, but while I was at the church in Linden, the college at Wake Forest, North Carolina, moved to Winston-Salem, and the Baptist convention opened a new seminary, Southeastern, in Wake Forest. Dr. Stealey, professor of history at Southern Seminary, had been named its president.

While we were in Linden, we had attended the Baptist convention in Texas, where a pastor friend introduced me to Dr. Stealey. I mentioned to him that I was planning on attending seminary shortly. We did not know it, but God had arranged for me to meet one of his angels. Here are the details.

Dr. Stealey told me, "If you want a real challenge, come to our school. We don't have all the accommodations of our sister schools, so we'll have an uphill climb for a while. It will take strong-minded men and women to make it through the next few years with us."

He must have studied psychology. He told Mary Edna, "I believe you got grit enough to make it at Southeastern, but I don't know so much about your husband." He must have been joking, but what he said had the tone of something meaningful.

His invitation became a challenge. My wife and I had many discussions about where I should attend seminary, but the talk with the president clarified which school would be in our future. After all, the president of the seminary was a friend!

My call to missions made the need for seminary training a priority after resigning the Linden church.

After much prayer we accepted Dr. Stealy's school. Southeastern seminary at Wake Forest, North Carolina was our choice for the Fall semester.

The move to North Carolina went smoothly. Wake Forest had been a college town with many student apartments and some for families, and we found one with reasonable rent. The children were enrolled in school as we made Wake Forest our home and started making friends.

Finances were a concern, however. Necessities quickly ate into our savings to the extent that we had no money for heating oil. We needed to do something quickly. I decided to talk to Dr. Stealey about getting a loan of $50 for heating oil. When he jokingly asked when I would be able to pay him back, I told him of the job I had before becoming a minister and that my priority at that point was to get a job.

He asked me about my pastoral experience, and I shared some of my life experiences with him. He suggested that I talk to a professor who found churches for students to pastor, and I did that as well. The professor told me that more than a a hundred students who had enrolled that fall were looking for work in churches as well and that they were on a long waiting list. I left knowing I had to do something about my family's finances.

Inwood Baptist Church

> Did I not tell you that if you believe, you will see the
> glory of God? (John 11:40)

It was time to pray. I planned to spend the next few days looking for a job. School did not start for two or more weeks. The rent had been paid, and we had enough food and gasoline. The $50 loan took care of our need for heating oil. We knew God was in control. Prayer had settled our concerns. Jackie and Arthur were happy children, and we felt calm about our future.

Then it happened. The telephone rang. The professor I had spoken to about church work told me he had gotten a call from a church committee asking about a young Alabama student who had just moved to Wake Forest. They had given him my my name and wanted to meet with me.The professor said he would call the committee and arrange a meeting for seven-thirty that evening.

That prompted an all-hands-on-deck frantic preparation mode. We wondered: *How did that group know about our move to Wake Forest? Who gave the professor my name?* We knew no one in North Carolina. Despite our frenzied questions, we felt God's overwhelming presence. The Holy Spirit reminded us of the seminary president's suggestion that I talk with that professor. We realized this had been God's work.

Consider the following. There was absolutely no church that needed a pastor earlier in the day, but a church committee had called the seminary with my name. That was all due to my having met Dr. Stealey in a Texas parking deck!. The hardest and coldest unbeliever could not deny the providence of God working through someone He had used as His angel.

The evening with the Pulpit Committee was memorable. I asked right away, "How did you get my name?" Someone said he had read a three-line item in the North Carolina Baptist weekly paper that had mentioned that the pastor of the Linden Baptist Church had just enrolled in Southeastern Seminary in preparation for missionary service. The article mentioned an award I had received for my success in the church with a group of men known as the Church Brotherhood.

The Pulpit Committee came from a church in a semi-rural area outside Raleigh. The North Carolina State University is on Raleigh's outskirts near the church.

In that two-hour meeting, we went over every aspect of our family and church life. The committee seemed satisfied and asked if I would be available to preach on Sunday.

I answered in the affirmative, but then I said something bold: "I'll preach for you, but if you're going to give me a call for service, you'll have to expedite the process. We've just moved, and I need a job. I was going tomorrow to look for work." They assured me that they would make their decision quickly.

After the service on Sunday, the committee extended the call for me to become pastor of the Inwood Baptist Church. The call was accepted and presented to the church who accepted the committee's recommendation. We moved to the church pastorium, assuming the new work the Lord had provided. From south Alabama to south Raleigh. It was the work of a loving Father.

Inwood Baptist Church's pastoral home was about three hundred yards from the church. On the first Sunday church members offered to move us to our new home. We accepted and they moved us using a large open-bed truck. During the move our ironing board was lost. The following Sunday we found three ironing boards on our porch.

God had plans for Inwood Baptist Church to be a blessing to more than one seminary student. During the time I spent as pastor at Inwood, three other students came to assist in ministry, and the church helped them meet their financial and personal needs while they were in school.

The second level of the church home was unfinished. Two students who would help in ministry at Inwood needed a place to stay. The church paid to have the second floor finished for them and did not charge them rent.

God's plan always covers every need of the faithful if they are willing to join Him in the labor needed to follow it. His plans are for all His servants. His love through those who serve Him blesses His children and many who need to be reborn children in redemption. It is His love and plan for their obedient lives!

Camden Baptist Church

> Be still before the Lord and wait patiently for him.
> (Psalm 37:7)

The wonderful people at Inwood were ideally suited to help me, a young pastor, finish my master's degree at Southeastern Seminary. Graduation was ahead with a missionary assignment to a country yet to be named.

Our two children had been blessed with exceptional love and care. Mary Edna had been able to take in some studies at the seminary. She also helped with the finances by working at a medical center for the mentally impaired.

She was shaken when she arrived home one morning having worked from eleven at night until seven in the morning. One patient was being moved from one detention area to another and decided she wanted a handful of Mary Edna's hair. She said, "The Lord sure took care of me last night. It could have been a sad situation if God had not sent someone to check on me during the time of the move." God's angels work for His children in every moment of need!

As graduation approached, I spent time in chapel each morning in solemn thought about the future. We would be leaving a church that had blessed us beyond measure, relocating while in preparation for overseas ministry, and saying goodbye to student friends. The chapel gave time to think of these matters, but mostly, it was a time of prayer and inspiration. It was exceptionally meaningful in the last days. That made what happened next an example of God's grace in our lives.

After chapel on a day of the last week of school, a gentleman whose name was prominent among Baptists came to talk. We went to a small room in the chapel meant for private prayer. He told me he was from the Southern Baptist Foreign Mission Board. It seemed strange someone would make a trip from Richmond, Virginia to Wake Forest, North Carolina to speak to me. He was hesitant about addressing why he wanted to meet with me. He said that the board had concerns about an overseas assignment for me. In fact, he said there would be no appointment. Tears were in his eyes as he said that. Bringing the message had become very personal for him; he had thought about all the time I had been preparing for such an assignment. He did not know why the board had made that decision. He said he had simply been told to tell me about it so I could make other plans.

The news shocked me. I would not have entered seminary or planned to resign from Linden Baptist if I had not felt the call to overseas missions. After several minutes of quiet reflection, I told him, "Thank you for your deep concern. God's plan for us speaks to this moment. After following what I felt in faith to be His will, I am still blessed. I finished my seminary education, which is necessary for ministry. Now, as God leads in another direction, it will be in service He has planned. We have a wonderful church. While we are disappointed, the call to overseas missions is still in effect for us. You have been God's messenger to tell us of His way forward. I'll always remember your personal concern in this matter."

My visitor was pleased with my response, and he left. It was time for me to pray and think on the matter. The chapel was empty, but God seemed to be there with me, and I needed His guidance.

When something occurs that changes your immediate plans, it opens the way for times of reflective prayer. The one thing that would not change was my firm belief that this was God's plan for us. Responding to His will is always satisfying. It would make my graduation even more of an opportunity to seek His will.

I explained this to my family and told them I did not know why the board had decided not to send me. I remembered the doctors telling me that I had bad blood; I thought that might have been the case since I had met all the other requirements for missionary work abroad.

I put on hold my plan to resign as pastor of Inwood as we made new plans. Several matters required my attention. The church needed more land to expand as new, young families had joined the church and the demand for space was urgent.

We had developed a friendship with the owner of a large plantation-type cattle farm facing the church. He was president of the local golf club and had made me an honorary member; I played on the course at no cost. It was fitting to continue working with him as he had learned of our rental of three of his small cottages for Sunday school classes. He was disturbed we had been charged and refunded the rent. The superintendent of his farm was a church deacon. My additional time was spent in attending to these matters. My friend owned the land behind our church. He gave it to us without cost. The new education building unit could now be built.

Two weeks after graduation, we were thinking about God's plan for our future. There were times of prayer each day concerning where God would lead us.

Usually at church services, newcomers would sit with those who had invited them, so seldom did I see people I did not recognize. On one Sunday, however, I saw four men sitting on the back row. There were no members with them.

After worship and a time of fellowship, I spoke to the members of the congregation as they left. The four men stayed behind and asked to speak to me. They told me they were from Camden Baptist Church in Camden, Alabama, the seat of Wilcox County. They assumed I had never heard of their church. That opened a conversation as to its size and other matters they thought were important.

The burning question Mary Edna and I had was what they were doing in Raleigh on a Sunday morning. They said, "We've come to talk with you about becoming our pastor."

Mary Edna and I asked many questions: How had they learned about our remote church? Had they known our time in seminary was in preparation for overseas ministry? Who told them there had been no resignation since graduation? How could they travel this far without contacting us as to our availability that day?

The men smiled as they listened to our questions. They had read of my graduation in the Alabama Baptist weekly paper. The article mentioned our present location and previous pastorates. Camden and Linden were in the same area of Alabama. It is possible they had learned of our work there.

If one doubts the providence of God for those who seek to follow His plan, here is a wonderful example of how God leads. Strangely, the article did not mention my reason for leaving Linden and attending seminary. If that had been mentioned, the four would not have traveled over six hundred miles to speak with me. When I shared my reason for attending seminary, they seemed disappointed.

When I told them about the visit I had had with a member of the mission board, the atmosphere changed. It was time for prayer. After we talked with our Lord together, the men asked if we would make plans to come to Camden one weekend to preach and meet the people. In consideration of their prayers, their long trip, and the need for God's direction for the future, we agreed. A trip to visit the church would give us an indication of the will of God.

Many call this a trial sermon, but we felt it would be more for our benefit than for theirs. We needed to know God's will for our future; that would serve them and us. The church needed to hear and meet a prospective pastor, and I needed to know if I would be pleasing God by accepting the new pastorate.

Think for a moment. Two weeks prior to that Sunday, we did not know what the future held for us, but then four men traveled for ten hours to hear a preacher they had no assurance would be in the pulpit. They knew nothing of the situation concerning missions or the needs of the pastor. It was a venture based on faith that God was leading, and they had followed out of obedience to Him. Four men had become angels of God and opened the way for two of His servants to follow His leading. The most unbelieving would have to agree that no man could plan such activities. There is no rational reasoning in the entire matter. Thus, God led the Green family to move to Camden. Senator Jeff Sessions was at that time a high school student in the city. Kay Ivey, a future governor of Alabama, was sixteen then, and she and her family attended the church. Her father directed our Sunday school, and her mother worked in our bank.

It was a time of turmoil in Selma, a place frequented by Dr. Martin Luther King. When continuing his mission, Dr. King would visit Camden. These visits and our work with town officials in maintaining order with a modicum of peace made clear why God had led us to Camden. It was a tremendous learning experience with daily challenges.

The state senator for Wilcox County, who owned an automobile dealership, attended Camden Baptist. We were two of several who dealt with daily town issues. On one occasion, we met with Governor George Wallace to discuss the location and use of junior colleges in Alabama. After our discussion, the governor told me, "As a politician, you should make a good Baptist preacher." He was Methodist, but my ideas as to how students and teachers should be accommodated did not register well with him.

One afternoon, the senator called asking to come to his automobile agency. When we sat down to talk, he pointed to a group that had gathered on the lawn at the rear of the courthouse across the street from his agency. He explained why he had called me with a certain panic in his voice. The crowd had gathered to do bodily harm to a man who had returned to Camden after several years' absence. The senator felt they might hang the man if something was not done.

The man had lived in Camden with two elderly sisters while writing a thesis on small-town organizations, people, and politics. Camden was well organized with proud people and politics affected by generational likes and dislikes of public persons and politicians. The senator told me that the man had written several unacceptable things about certain people he had met in Camden. Not having read the man's book, we knew nothing of the offense, but it was obviously a problem for those who had gathered.

The senator and I addressed the crowd; we wanted to avoid anything bad happening that might make the national news. None of the men on the lawn could explain what the man had written in his thesis. They said that they "had heard" several women talking about it. We asked them if anyone realized the implications personally and for the town if some ungodly act was performed to fatally wound the subject. This was a friendly confrontation that resulted in a meaningful response. The group remained on the lawn but seemed much calmer. We agreed that the writer would stay where he had lived in Camden until the Senator could arrange for the highway patrol to escort him to the airport for a flight back to his hometown, St. Louis.

I talked with the man who had been in danger, and he made a shocking remark: "I now know how Jesus felt." That remarked touched my heart. I said, "No sir, you do not know how Jesus felt. He suffered for men to be forgiven of their sins. He died that the ungodly could be made right with God. Your actions have proven just the opposite. Never again compare yourself to Jesus. He never sinned. You have a lawn full of men across the street who believe you have sinned against them. You need Jesus's forgiveness like the rest of us."

After silently talking with God, the one who thought he had been a victim was given instructions how to get back to where he was staying and wait for the highway patrol to escort him to the airport in Montgomery.

I faced other challenges in the years spent with God's people in Camden, but having been in the military twice, I was able to meet them with God's power and love.

Camden Baptist worshiped in a wooden-frame building that seated two hundred or more, but it was outdated. There was room enough for a new auditorium structure. The deacons and the church agreed it was time for a new building for worship.

The church elected one man and mine women to choose an architect. The man serving on that board owned a large plantation and a company that sold seed to buyers all over America. He was a trustee of Howard College and on the committee at the Alabama Baptist Convention office that handled the ministers' retirement funds.

The Alabama Baptist Convention had built a new convention office, and the Camden deacon was a member of the committee that had been responsible for its construction. A close friend who had dated a Camden girl when young had been the architect.

The group recommended two architects. The deacon recommended the architect of the Convention building in Montgomery. He asked for 10 percent of the total cost of the building to be paid to him after he finished his drawings and before construction began.

Other ministers who had buildings recently built for their churches were asked about the architects they used, and several gave glowing recommendations of a Birmingham architect. They said he would not ask for money until construction began and after the church received money borrowed for the job. His name was given to the committee for consideration.

Not having raised money for the project, the committee felt that the Birmingham firm was the one it would use. The deacon and one woman were the only to vote for the Montgomery firm. After the vote, the deacon erupted. In an angry tone, he made all manner of accusations about the selection of the other architect. His tirade lasted over ten minutes. The women were visibly embarrassed. They had high respect for the one who was addressing the pastor with rough accusations; their love for both caused them inner conflict.

To the relief of everyone, the vote was registered, the committee finished its work, and the result would be presented to the church. As it called for no funds, it would be passed without much if any discussion.

The pastoral residence was across the street from the church. After the meeting adjourned it was time for quiet prayer. My study was rather secluded from the rest of the house. Going straight to that quiet place, I sat in the dark and talked with my Heavenly Father more than thirty minutes.

Later, I called the deacon. What I told him is as vivid today as it was that night. The Holy Spirit of our Lord had spoken. The emphasis was not to restore friendship, but that would have been appreciated. No, it was to follow what God makes central in the life of every believer, the reason for the cross of Jesus Christ, the basis of life for those who will serve Him. It is the love of God revealed in Jesus Christ.

I told the deacon, "Sir, I want to thank you for your faithfulness to our Lord. It has been deeply impressive how you work with us here at church and across the state. You have had our prayers. There is one thing responsible for this call. It is the love of God. I am your pastor. I love you now and will love you unconditionally as we serve the Lord together. Please rest well tonight. Say a prayer for me, for our church. Remember, I love you. Goodnight."

I did not wait for his response. In the following days, it was if there had never been a matter of concern. In fact, two weeks later, the deacon's wife called and told Mary Edna that they had two extra tickets to the Auburn versus Georgia football game, and she asked us to join them. God's love never fails!

If there is a belief in the providence of God with His plan prevailing in daily life, the basis for it must be honored and practiced. God's love is the key to opening doors, mending hearts, and developing faithfulness. His Spirit makes it real in daily life and moments of crises. Angels are at work by the will of God for those who love those they serve while honoring God's name and purpose and following His will.

Indialantic Baptist Church

You are my help and deliverer, Lord. (Psalm 71:5)

One never knows when God is going to give guidance for change of service stations in the kingdom. Changes that affect family and church are a result of prayer, and they always come with the assurance they are of God. When one feels that the work being done needs to be turned over to another, God makes the change. Here is how it occurred with us.

Plans for the new building were completed, and the senior deacon would be in control of construction. The money had become available. Camden had been the target of some very popular organizers and exploiters during the racial crises, but that had passed, and church attendance had increased. Having worked with the mayor, sheriff, probate judge, city council, and leaders of other churches in maintaining peace and an honorable status for the town and county, I felt God had been leading us. All matters had not been settled positively or in what could be felt like God's will for the day, but there were no hanging issues.

The nominating committee of the church began choosing leaders for the coming year. After all the days of unrest and being the target of some unwanted activities, the interest of the members was not internal; it was not on the work of God in the church.

After prayer at Sunday dinner, I told Mary Edna I had a deep feeling that our work there was finished. Being one who loved deeply and changed locations with difficulty, she gave me a cold stare. That was one reason any move had to be of God rather than a quick decision on my part. I asked her to pray about our need for change as the church began the construction of new facilities.

A week later, one of my wife's close friends asked her, "Is there something wrong?" Feeling Mary Edna had mentioned it brought the need for a talk. She assured me she had not spoken of our feelings; she asked, "How did she know?" We learned years before that God's Spirit has a way of going before us as well as being in us. It should never be taken for granted that the leading of God is only for leaders.

The church at Camden had been wonderfully faithful to our Lord. The congregation was on the verge of having a beautiful building that would lead to a great opportunity for growth. Making a change with a new worship center, the church had much to offer a new pastor. The church had known growth in the past six years. We were confident this was God's providential plan for our lives.

A week later, a telephone call confirmed why we felt led to think of changing leadership at Camden. Two years prior, a new church in Florida had asked us to preach a revival. On the phone was a man my two brothers had worked for when delivering newspapers in Birmingham years before. He said he was the chairman of the Pulpit Committee for the Indialantic Baptist Church.

The pastor who had founded the church was deeply loved by the members. It was shocking for them to hear the need for a new pastor. The church had the use of a school to start the church in a small town near its present location. The congregation had built a new sanctuary and Sunday school building since our time with them.

The chairman said his pastor had been in an automobile accident that had affected his ability to talk. He would not recover with a voice strong enough to preach. The caller said that the pastor could not finish his sermons and needed the help of a deacon to close the service.

Then came the shock. The chairman said, "Brother Green, our committee met tonight. We voted to ask you to become our pastor!" He said the committee felt the church would honor its decision. Heavy emphasis had been put on the fact I had preached for them for a week two years before. That was as unorthodox as I could imagine. I told him of the need to visit the church.

After agreeing on a suitable date for me to preach, Mary Edna and I visited the Indialantic Baptist Church of Indialantic, Florida. The church was beautiful! They had spared no cost when building the sanctuary. Because I had been there previously, the congregation was very receptive to our message. Mary Edna and I had the impression that God was in the meeting.

Arriving home, we knew it was time for prayer. After several days of prayer and discussion we decided if a call was extended to us, we would accept it. The church gave the call. I resigned the Camden Baptist Church and became the pastor of First Baptist, Indialantic.

My ministry at Indialantic Baptist Church lasted twelve years during which time more than fifty souls were called to vocational work in the kingdom of God. In His plan for the church and us was a divine union formed by the providence of God.

Seoul International Baptist Church

> Commit to the Lord whatever you do, and he will establish your plans. (Psalm 16:3)

The Florida Baptist Convention gave an invitation for pastors to attend a special conference in Tampa, and I accepted. It was always a joy to be with fellow pastors from around the state. Inspiration for local work and information from others in the work helped in planning and preaching.

Jo Ann Shelton, a professor of music at Southwestern Seminary in Fort Worth, Texas, sang at each session of the meeting. She made such a tremendous impression on me that I asked her to come sing at First Baptist in Indialantic. She said she would come and offered to lead a Bible study for the women of the church as well.

When the time arrived, there was a great interest in the meeting. Jo Ann had been the featured singer on the Sunday radio program known as The Baptist Hour. No one could remember when a visitor taught the women in a Bible study. We were informed the study would be from Revelation, a book that requires deep study. The women responded in great numbers to the Bible study, which preceded Jo Ann's evening concert.

Jo Ann sang to a full house each evening. Her concerts focused on our Lord and His blessings for believers. At the close of the third evening of music, she sang, "So Send I You." At that moment, she became one of God's angels.

It was one of the few times Mary Edna sat with me in church. When the singing stopped, something happened in my heart. God had spoken. Leaning over to my wife, I said, "God has renewed our call to missions. I will share it with the church tonight." She asked quietly, "Tonight?" I nodded.

I stood before the congregation, which was expecting a benediction, and my words simply flowed. "Tonight, as Jo Ann sang her invitation hymn, God spoke to me. He just renewed our call to the mission field. Usually, the deacons and personnel team members would be notified. Tonight is an exception. You came to hear a beautiful concert that has stirred our hearts. You will go home knowing your pastor just resigned in response to God's renewal of a call."

The people were silent, in shock. After the closing prayer, a few women from the missionary group came to say they would pray for us. Others did not seem to know what to say. They had had one previous pastor; my ministry had lasted thirteen years, and for many, I was the only pastor they had known.

Making my resignation public with the purpose of serving overseas galvanized the membership; they supported the move. We had volunteered for missionary work when we were thirty, and then, we were fifty-three. God's plan and providence made His ministry a wonderful journey. A look back revealed how we had received the love and assistance of God's people. We recalled how the Holy Spirit had led us which brought memories of God's glory amid difficulties and trials. Here are a few activities that reveal His providential love as His plan unfolded in ministry.

The geographic location of the Indialantic Baptist Church was critical. It was about a fifteen-minute drive from Melbourne High. The Florida Institute of Technology was in Melbourne. The students of both schools had to cross the Indian River to reach the beach. To the north, Satellite Beach High School was the same distance and was convenient to the beach. Great numbers of students from the three schools were on the beach daily. The Kennedy Space Center, twenty miles north of Indialantic, was deeply involved in putting a man on the moon. The largest technology firm in Florida was twenty minutes south of the church. Many who joined the church were employed by one of those two.

We were blessed to have dedicated Christians to join us in our efforts. An example was Colonel Marc Ducote, supervisor of the Titan Three-C missile program, who was our Sunday school director. He was as dedicated to the church as he was to his government work. Many of the members worked at the Marshall Space Center. President Kennedy had challenged them to put a man on the moon. Few pastors know what their congregants face in the working world. My congregants who worked at the Marshall Space Center needed to unwind on the Lord's Day; they needed inspiration for the work ahead, which brought the threat of failure. We were asked to pray with them especially about the moon launch. All of us were greatly blessed to see that successful moon launch, which we witnessed standing in our yard.

The church had provided me a wonderfully effective staff. It was a mark of God's direction. They led to noticeable church growth.

We retired the bonds we had sold to construct our house of worship. A new education building provided a modern kitchen and area for informal meetings and a place of fellowship each week when meals were served.

The beach was within walking distance of the church, so young beachgoers became a mission target for the church. The church blended with the community. The challenge came to provide a gathering place on the beach. The city council rented to us for one dollar an old restaurant building on the beach located between a hotel that had closed and an office building no longer in use.

The deacons and staff of the church along with interested members reworked the interior, which we named the Son & Fish. On many nights, music groups sang gospel songs as entertainment. The students decorated the tables that had been big wire spools., Water and soft drinks were served. There was also a pool table.

It was evident each night that God was doing something great in His kingdom. The youth choir of the church planned an outdoor concert for a Sunday afternoon on the beach that a large group of students and residents attended. After the concert, the choir members took time to sit with those attending to share Jesus Christ.

The church approved of a youth evangelist to come for several nights during the first summer of the beach work. We had arranged for the speaker to stand on the back of a huge flatbed truck and broadcast his message over some speakers to those on the beach.

There was evidence the hand of God was active in this endeavor. When the truck did not arrive, word came that there had been an accident; the truck was in a ditch. A huge crowd had gathered in response to the advertising for the evening event. Rather than disappoint the young people, our men chose to use the flat top of the old restaurant building. When the sound equipment was put in place up there, the preacher was heard for a great distance. It was a huge success. We agreed that this was a work of God. Our plans had failed, but He had had a better plan.

One of the shining examples of God's work involved a young student from Finland. The high school principal at Satellite Beach was the father of a seventeen-year-old son. Having heard of the availability of exchange students, they inquired and booked one to come live with them for a year. His name was Yari Honkikari.

On the first Sunday morning, Yari came to church. His greeting at the door after worship was in halting English. He said, "Christ … is Lord … in Florida … *and* … in Finland!" This made a lasting impression. We bonded that day at the church door!

Yari asked us to join him in prayer for his father, who had become gravely ill, and we did. Two weeks later, he came to our home and said he wanted us to pray about his situation. He wanted to return home to be with his mother during the time of crisis. He said his finances were short; that was hindering his going home. We prayed, and as we finished praying, the telephone rang. The caller was the owner of a nearby automobile agency who had family in Finland and had met Yari. He asked if Yari was with me. He wanted to speak to him.

After their conversation, Yari had tears in his eyes. He said, "Pastor, we need to pray a prayer of thanksgiving. He has arranged a flight home for me and back after the crisis with my father passes."

During a time of looming sadness, that young man had found the joy and peace that only a loving God could provide through one of His angels. When thinking of God's providence and the work of those who become His angels, believers must pause to say, "Praise God!"

Later, Yari became a worker in the Lutheran Church of Finland and arranged a preaching tour for us. Sixteen members of our church spent ten days in Finland. There were fifteen speaking and worship times. One was in Helsinki in the largest church in Finland. That happened because a seventeen-year-old Finnish boy believed God was His Lord and Savior in Jesus Christ. We must never forget that God's providence is for all believers who follow His plan for life!

At times, events challenge conscious reality. There was an immediate reaction to our resignation from the Indialantic Baptist church. The people responded as God's people do when they are inspired. Requests for our time overwhelmed us. The response was because of what God had done for His church and how He had used the two of us and our children in His service. It is to His glory as to how it was to end in Florida.

When the Mission Board learned of our request for a mission appointment, it gave us a positive response. They sent the necessary documents, which we quickly completed and returned. The physical exams that were required of us revealed no serious need for concern. It was exactly the opposite of our experience twenty-three years earlier after my first physical exam. We then had an interview with the group that would approve the appointment. Earlier, our request had been denied prior to such a meeting with the reviewing board.

As we waited to be called for the interview, the board gave us an option. We received the names of the countries and the places needing missionaries with our qualifications. It was to be in work using English. The names of each country with a current need were on separate cards in a bag, and Mary Edna and I considered a few places to be interesting, and we discussed them. We felt this would take several days of thought and prayer. After reading the cards, Mary Edna shook the bag. One card fell to the floor. Picking it up, she said, "This one seems like a message from the Lord." It was South Korea!

We had visited Korea with thirty pastors on a trip to assist our missionaries in a very intense crusade, and it had been fascinating. We worked with our missionaries and many leading Korean Christians. At a mass rally for the military, God reached out to us in a very unusual way. Twenty-five hundred officers and men squatted on the landing strip of a military airport, and the visiting pastors sat in chairs and were joined by several generals and Korean pastors. The group sat near a gazebo equipped for those who would bring the rally messages. The military men were two hundred yards from the gazebo.

Billy Kim, the interpreter for the internationally televised Billy Graham crusade, had become the civilian-military chaplain. He had several radio stations broadcasting into China. The military rally was his project. He was to be the featured speaker. A few days before, we had been with him at a Youth for Christ meeting in Seoul.

As Dr. Kim started to the gazebo, he stopped, touched me on the shoulder, and said, "Come on. I want you to preach for us." All servants of God have read about being ready to preach at any time, but it seemed like a general warning, not a bomb.

The morning of the rally, Mary Edna and I had read in our daily devotion, "No one serving as a soldier gets entangled in civilian affairs, but rather tries to please his commanding officer" (2 Timothy 4:2a, 2:4). This was God's preparation for such a time as this. His providence must never be questioned.

I interpreted the verses from Paul to a young preacher, Timothy, as a challenge to the soldiers to give God first place in their lives in total allegiance regardless of their circumstances. I said Christians were faithful to their countries and those who led them. Soldiers devoted to Jesus Christ in repentance and faith would have great lives here and in the hereafter.

More than two hundred responded. Standing around the gazebo, Pastor Kim told them how to become Christians. Most had been raised as Buddhists and had never experienced an invitation to become Christian. Later, their names and units were given to a chaplain for follow-up.

Remembering our Korean experiences made our decision much easier concerning where we would spend time in our Lord's service. As we prayed, the decision became clear and final; we would ask to be considered for South Korea, and the division monitoring such appointments seemed greatly satisfied. God gets the glory for having prepared the way for His call to have a positive response. It may have been many years in completion, but it was as clear and valid as the first time it was made by God.

The work of God at Pentecost revealed how a call is made. Circumstances and needs have changed, but the Holy Spirit does for servants today what He did for the apostles. They were changed from followers to leaders in kingdom work. They had matured as believers and were then ready for God's call. God goes before the one called to make clear that the response can be made without fear and with a certainty that removes doubts. That was our experience.

A few weeks after we gave our decision to the board, we went for a final interview on a glorious day that we, excited servants of God, had envisioned many years before.

When going before the review board for our final interview, we received another shock. While I was pastor at Indialantic, I had been appointed to the convention's committee on boards. One of the vacancies we filled for the International Missions Board was for a trustee who was sitting on the committee to interview me! We quietly praised God for His providential care in that matter. The review board approved our request for mission work in Korea. We were told to report to Callaway Gardens Resort in Georgia, where we and other volunteers would be prepared for work abroad. As it was a resort site, cabins were very suitable for couples. We had meals at the resort buffet.

We had classes daily with qualified teachers who spent many hours training us for new lifestyles. It was very informative, but seldom were classes designed for the special work in an English-language church. We were the only ones in the group with that field assignment, so that gave me ample time to play golf. Orientation was a delight!

At graduation, the board gave us our specific assignment—the

Seoul International Baptist Church. This was followed by a formal recognition service by the board. Our arrival on the field of service would be January 1, 1980.

We were limited in what we could take to a specific list of goods. Word came to us that a member of Shades Mountain Baptist Church in Birmingham would use his company's facilities to load and seal our shipping crate and send it to the proper shipping company at no cost to us. This was an unexpected blessing. He was our shipping agent during the entire time of our Korean service. He was another angel of God!

Going to Korea was an adventure. Our aging parents had mixed emotions; our leaving the country was much different from going to another state. It was a test of faith; we had to trust the Lord with our future. We spent as much time as possible with our parents before leaving for Korea.

As my sister and some of her family were living in Alaska, we booked a flight with a layover there, and we enjoyed three days of reunions and snow sledding. It was a great break for two who had lived in a rush for many days in preparation for overseas service.

We were booked on a late-night flight to Korea. The Korean flight agency in the terminal was closed. When we were boarding the plane, a station agent helped with our baggage. The plane's baggage compartment door was frozen shut, so our baggage was placed in the first-class area.

After many hours, we landed in Korea. The missionaries of Korea always met new workers on arrival. After clearing customs, we walked from the station. There were no missionaries. The Korean flight facility in Alaska had not sent the flight manifest to Korea. Our future friends in service had contacted the Korean airport manager. He informed them that he had no Greens on the list of passengers arriving from Alaska. They left thinking we had not been on the plane, and we had no idea where to go or how to get there. But God helps those who follow His plan for them.

We looked around for someone to help us and were shocked to see Colonel Jimmy Arrington and his wife, Mildred, members and workers in our Florida church. Jimmy taught a large Bible class on Wednesday evenings. Our church was near an army facility, so many military men with families worshiped with us. To this day, I do not remember how these two angels of God learned of our arrival. We later learned that he had been sent to Korea while we were going through orientation.

The Arringtons knew where we needed to go. Fellow missionaries at the missionary office were startled when they saw us. They explained their reason for leaving the airport, and it was never mentioned again.

We were escorted to our living quarters in a three-story apartment building, one of many in the area, which was called the housing compound. It was surrounded by a fence, and a Korean family manned the gate. That was our home for the next twelve years.

The church, the Seoul International Baptist Church, had not had an assigned pastor in nearly four years. The mission, which managed the affairs of Korean missionaries, had assigned a missionary to be an interim pastor.

The church met on the third floor of a building on Yoido, an island in the Han River. The Korean congress and state television station studio and headquarters were also on the island, which was connected to the mainland by a huge concrete bridge.

The church, known as SIBC to missionaries, had a live-in custodial family. Security had been a major need after the Korean war; stealing had become a national plague, and security measures were evident throughout the country.

Missionaries had made a major impact on society by distributing food and clothing to those in need. As the country recovered, the door was open to God's work.

Korea's national religion was Buddhism. The country had moved toward democracy having previously been a monarchy. A president and elected congressional members were leading the country in our time in Korea.

The United States had 35,000 soldiers in Korea when we arrived. The Seoul military post was one of their largest of several military bases throughout the country. The military chapel in Seoul was not equipped or staffed for the families of service members. For this and other reasons, many of the military came to worship at SIBC. The chairman of deacons was the commanding officer of all marines assigned to Korea.

Once a year, the military brought troops and equipment from various places for joint maneuvers with the South Korean military. The church decided to make its facilities available as sleeping quarters for some field units, which was better for them than bivouac living. A medical unit from Hawaii stayed for a week with us.

We shared with the troops how our Lord had met every need for life. Jokingly, we told the soldiers that they could tell their home folks they were spending a great deal of time in church.

The country was full of factories producing products for foreign companies. Representatives of these companies became members of SIBC, an English-language church. One Sunday, people representing twenty countries attended worship.

Missionaries who wanted their children to be in Sunday school also became part of our congregation. A multitude of Koreans who learned English in their schools but had never heard it spoken joined them.

The Koreans who were converted to Christianity became supremely versed in the bible and were extremely dependable servants of the Lord Jesus Christ. When we arrived in Korea, approximately 15 percent of Koreans were Christian. When we left after twelve years, more than 25 percent had converted.

An explanation of growth was evident in every effort of SIBC. It was manifest in ways beyond our planning or thoughts. On one occasion, Mr. Kim, a Korean pharmacist, came to the church office. He had a plan for evangelistic work in a prison whose warden was a former Christian minister and his friend. But an English-language church working in a Korean prison seemed to be a stretch. The visitor said that if SIBC would join him, he would get permission and plan for a time of worship for the inmates on a Sunday afternoon. The message would be interpreted if a missionary fluent in Korean could be enlisted.

It was suggested that the choir would be an asset if its members were willing to help in the effort.

When others learned that the pharmacist used the proceeds from his business to provide for worship in a prison, many gladly responded. It was to be a new experience for most as they had never been in a prison.

There were two key results in this effort. The prisoners, ages eighteen to twenty-eight, responded in great numbers. Mr. Kim took the new converts under his personal Bible training to equip them for Christian life. Twice monthly he was permitted to get those who made professions of faith to come to a discipling class he conducted. The prison environment made this a critical need.

When he completed the discipling, he sent word to SIBC to prepare for a baptismal service. There was a small, three-foot-deep pool in the prison used for washing prisoners' clothes. The warden gave permission for the use of the pool.

At the first baptismal service, there were 135 prisoners baptized. Mr. Kim had several white robes available. Each candidate wore a robe and handed it to the next candidate. The shallow pool with young men who had never witnessed a baptismal service made for a long but glorious afternoon.

The second result of a ten-year prison ministry revealed the direction of God's work in Korea. In those ten years, more than a thousand prisoners were baptized as Christians.

Mr. Kim took each one when he was released from prison to his hometown. Prior to release, he would inform a Christian minister in the area of the impending arrival of the new converts. Introducing released prisoners to the ministers had tremendous positive results.

The traditional rate of return to prison was 85 percent for released prisoners, but in ten years of evangelization ministry with Mr. Kim, not one released prisoner was returned for committing another crime. That was the stunning result of one man's vision. Mr. Kim was God's angel at work!

The dedication of converted Koreans to Christianity was greater than what I had ever experienced. At the close of worship one Sunday, an usher found a very unusual gift in the offering plate—a ring. He gave it to me and said that he had no idea who had given it. I thought of those who had attended that service, and a young Korean couple stood out in my mind. They always came after others were seated and sat in the back row, and they were always the first to leave; they seldom waited to speak to me.

The following Sunday as they were rushing to the door, I stopped them and asked if I could talk with them for a few minutes, and they agreed to that. In my office, I showed them the ring and asked if they recognized it. There was silence as both dropped their heads as if to say yes.

I asked, "Could you tell me why it was in the offering last Sunday?" The husband said, "Sir, we feel called to be missionaries when our training is completed. In prayer recently, we felt that our giving to the Lord was not enough. So as we held hands, she slipped off her ring and said, 'Let's give this.'"

I had never seen such godly dedication; my tears flowed. I joined their hands and slipped the ring on her finger. I said, "As long as we remember this, we will praise God for you two and pray for your ministry." It was a sacred vow that is being kept as this is written. Two of God's angels had blessed one who had never seen the dedication of this magnitude.

God was being honored by those who were new to Christianity in every phase of His work. I was asked to preach in a revival, and preparing for that was a new experience. Those who were involved showed total commitment to the revival, and it was a learning experience for my wife and me.

I was asked as a visiting preacher to join a group including two women and a man for house visits. They all had tasks when they entered someone's house. They removed their shoes upon entering, and one woman would go to the kitchen to see if she could relieve the wife or cook. The other woman would speak to the wife about the visit. The man, the interpreter, arranged the seating, which was cushions on the floor. The visitors and those of the home sat in a circle.

In a revival effort, a group was formed. After visiting several homes and an apartment complex, time for the evening worship was approaching. When this was mentioned, one of the women began speaking loudly about a visit she had planned. She was adamant as to the need. The man said she had promised we would come to the home of her friend. We decided to make the visit.

When the woman came to the door, she was holding a six-year old boy who looked feverish. After introductions, the group entered the home and began to share how God in Christ had a plan for every life.

Before we finished sharing our introduction to the Christian life, the mother interrupted us; boldly asking, "Can we pray now?" It was obvious that her friend had shared Christ with her, and the mother had been waiting for our visit to make it a personal experience. In prayer, the mother was strong in her confession and acceptance of Jesus Christ as her Savior.

When finishing the prayer, the mother made a startling statement. Her hand stroked the head of her sleeping boy; she looked into his face and said, "God has healed this mother's heart and her son's head." Tears flowed. God had used a friend who kept her promise to bring spiritual salvation and a healing miracle. She was God's angel at work!

Through the Years

> The Lord has done great things for us, and we are filled with joy. (Psalm 126:3)

Baptizing the converts from the Ohatchee revival was a concern. With twenty-three converts of all ages to be baptized, there was uncertainty. It was our first baptismal service. Men of the church built steps so the candidates could enter the creek that bordered the town. When all preparations were made, the deacons notified me.

On the Sunday of the baptism, the idea came to me to get some help. Maybe the pastor who preached the revival would be available.

When we went to his home, his wife said he was at the church in a meeting. That eliminated baptismal help.

On the trip back to Ohatchee, we stopped at a four-way stop sign near the downtown area of Anniston. As I drove through the intersection, I was hit on the driver's side by a large sedan. The collision pushed our car to the curb and against a power pole.

I climbed out of the car and saw a young boy sitting on the curb; he was bleeding. The driver did not seem to care about the boy, who we learned was his nephew. His face had hit the dashboard. We sat with him because no one seemed to notice his injury. People came to the scene, and we asked a woman to care for the boy.

The police arrived. One asked for our licenses and insurance verifications. As he looked at them, I asked if he would measure the long tire marks on the street. He did not seem interested. He said, "It looks like you ran a stop sign."

The intersection led to a hospital high on a hill. It seemed that the driver of the sedan had been going fast to make the climb when he hit us. The officers did not show interest in how the collision occurred. They were writing on documents to give to me.

The outlook was dim for the injured boy, me, and the cause of the accident. We learned why. The driver of the automobile that had hit us had been in the newspaper on the preceding Friday; he had been elected "The town's most eligible bachelor."

By then, a large crowd had gathered. When the leading officer of those present approached me to tell me his decision, I heard someone ask, "Jack, is that you?" I turned to see who had asked that, but he was in the back of the crowd. The sergeant saw him and yelled, "Mr. Bell, do you know this man?" In a loud voice, Mr. Bell answered, "Yes! I hired him on Friday." Everything came to a standstill. Mr. Bell was president of the largest bank in town. He was also on the board of trustees of Howard College. On Friday, they had approved me as the new alumni director. God had used a bank president as His angel.

An officer returned the credentials, saying that both of us had insurance and we could have our own vehicles repaired. The case was closed.

My old car still ran even with the side mashed in. It was not pretty to look at, but looks made no difference; a baptismal service was waiting for me.

A crowd had gathered at the creek to see church and family members baptized. It was a supremely important event for those being baptized. Many were concerned when they saw the condition of my car, but it was no time for explanations. I changed into my white baptismal clothing in my car and made my way to the creek. The mud and silt seemed very deep, but I found a flat rock to stand on.

The first to be baptized was a short and overweight man in his early twenties. We lowered him into the water. As he was being raised, I saw a snake in the roots of a tree next to the wooden stairs. I whispered to the man, "There's a snake in the roots of the tree by the steps. When you get out, find a stick and drive it off."

The man yelled, "Snake?" and waved around wildly; he actually hit me in the chest, and the blow knocked me off the flat rock into the silt. Men rushed to get me out of the mud, which was holding me fast.

After a tremendous automobile accident, the episode with the snake, and a dunk in the creek, the day finally ended. In reflection, I realized I had assurance that God meets the needs of those in His service. In the years ahead, I performed the sacred act of baptism many times, but none was more impressive than that day; nothing could stop God's blessings for a wonderful group of new Christians, not even a snake.

While I was serving in Linden, Alabama, I faced a tremendous negative response. The previous pastor had served for fifteen years but had failed to grow the church. That situation changed with one conversion. That was Johnny, the son of an important town leader, who had a tremendously bad reputation as the town drunk. Several of the members had told me of his well-known drunken fights. I tried to visit him at his home several times, but he would run and hide in the barn whenever he saw me pulling up. I talked to his wife, Bessie. She was proud of the heavy equipment business Johnny had built up and was proud of his work ethic, but she complained that he never wanted to go to church.

On one visit, I saw that next to the chair Johnny used in the front room was a small cutout in the wall. Later, we learned he would put his whiskey in a large container in the attic that had a hose attached to it that led to the cutout, which was covered by a small door. Johnny could fill his cup with whiskey by opening the door and releasing a rubber band on the hose. Bessie said he would do that every night until he stumbled off to bed.

It never bothered Johnny that he was drinking in a town that did not permit whiskey. While working on his heavy equipment digging pools for farmers, he learned of all the places it was sold illegally.

One evening, Johnny was on our hearts. Rather than park in front of his house, I parked out of sight. I had asked Bessie to announce to Johnny at exactly six o'clock, "I believe I see the preacher coming." We both knew what to expect if she gave the alarm.

I went around to the back door expecting to see Johnny exiting his house that way, and sure enough, it happened. He asked in a surprised tone, "What in the h*** are you doing here?"

When the shock was over, I told him the purpose of my visit. It was my first opportunity to tell Johnny how much God loved him. It is not appropriate for me to go into the details of our conversation, but in our first face-to-face meeting, God led Johnny to be comfortable talking to a preacher. However, it did not seem to make much of an impression. He said later that he had thought the conversation would be about his drinking. Of course, I had not mention drinking. I talked about his two wonderful children and what they needed as they grew. It was a short visit. He agreed to my request to pray for him. It was a meaningful visit.

The men of the church were enlarging the office space—moving walls and replacing the tile floor. After the men left one evening, it was time for me to make things usable for the next day. As I was preparing to leave there was a loud rapping on the door. I answered it. There was

Johnny Perry. He said, "Preacher, I need to talk to you right now." I considered that puzzling but satisfying.

Johnny said, "Preacher, tell me about being saved. I asked Bessie after your visit, but she said for me to come to ask you. So here I am. It was either go get drunk or come talk to you."

For more than thirty minutes, I explained the work of Jesus Christ through His crucifixion, death, and resurrection for the salvation of all. My final words from the Bible had to do with repentance. I told him that if he wanted to become a Christian, he needed God's forgiveness and a desire to change the way he lived. I said that he needed to ask God to completely remove the guilt of his past, to pray for cleansing, and vow to change himself.

Johnny asked, "Pastor, do you mean I just have to break down here on my knees and ask God for forgiveness?" I said yes. He and I slipped out of our chairs and got to our knees. Johnny began to weep. Then came the most complete repentance I could have ever imagined. It became clear why he was on his knees as he prayed. The remarks I had made at his home had gone to his heart. His prayer of repentance was not about whiskey; that seemed settled. It was to be able to ask God to bring salvation to his children.

I shared the glory of God with Johnny as a brother. He had some cows on acreage in the northern section of the county. He asked if I could go with him to see about a sick cow. In a country town, a preacher is asked to do many unusual things. When we arrived, the cow was not in the pasture. Entering the barn, Johnny said, "Here she is!" The cow was under the floor of the hay bin. Her legs were out in the breezeway. Johnny pulled the cow out from under the floor. We sat and stroked her. After some time, she moved. Johnny's cow was alive!

With times like these, we bonded as brothers for life. When there was a need for any hurting person, he would ask to go with me to minister. After sharing God's love with an unsaved person, Johnny would follow up. Many persons came to join the church declaring Jesus as Lord while being ushered down the aisle by Johnny.

In subsequent years, Johnny Perry was God's angel to me. We

hunted and fished together. We prayed together wherever we went. He became a prayer mate.

While serving in South Korea, Johnny wrote to me about Bessie's death: "Preacher, when I'm feeling sorry for myself because of Bessie's death, I do something you taught me. I just go down to the church and ask for the name of an unsaved person. Then I go visit that soul and tell him what Jesus did for me. It always lifts my spirit."

I remembered Johnny's words when Mary Edna went to be with the Lord. God's angel had prepared me for the days when it would have been so easy for me to feel sorrow for being alone.

This book has been all about how our Lord uses angels. It makes evident how God's providential care includes the helper and the helped. The remembrances were of parochial events, individuals, and churches.

The following is a revelation of God's providence that involves a nation. Korea became a divided nation after a civil war. Seoul became the capital of South Korea while Pyongyang was the capital of North Korea.

When war ceased, South Korea, with influence from the United States, became a democratic country. Progress in this direction became apparent in its developing commercial and international relationships.

The Seoul International Baptist Church had become well known. Having built a new auditorium and educational unit, the government had been involved. Permits and inspections were required.

The church had chosen to make the new facilities a memorial to a young woman who had died when Russia shot down a Korean airplane that had strayed over its territory. Her father was a deacon of our church.

At completion, SIBC held a dedication service in which government officials participated. The US ambassador to Korea gave the dedication message.

With this exposure, the government was fully aware of SIBC. Classes were held in the church for middle and high school Korean students. Many became converts to Christianity. When they made it public, their names were given to the Korean Baptist church, which was next to SIBC. When a student was baptized and joined that church, the family would usually follow and become members.

In a visit to the mission office, a missionary with many years in Korea made a request of me. "Jack, you've worked with college administrators, and I have a request." He gave me the name of a woman who was president of a large Korean college for women and asked me to send her a note of encouragement as she was home suffering from an illness. I wrote the note to her and gave it to the missionary to mail. I never expected the fallout from that note.

A few days after I wrote it, I heard a strange buzz on our apartment telephone. I mentioned that to a fellow missionary, who told me that my phone had been wiretapped. Other strange things happened. A black sedan followed me each day and night. There were two men in the car, but they never interfered with my daily activities. The custodial family who lived in the church annex said that two government officials had interviewed them for two hours. They wanted to know about my teaching and other personal matters. An employee at the mission office, a student in our night class, also had a long visit from the two men. The men asked her the same questions about me.

In the weeks preceding this, the government of South Korea had undergone a change. The elected president had been accused of wrongdoing, and the congressional body removed him from office.

A general of the army had been chosen to replace the president. The general was skeptical of the loyalty he would receive from those serving prior to his appointment. He placed the presidents of the schools and most of those serving the former president under house arrest.

I learned that the president of the women's college had never received my letter of encouragement. Mail sent to those under house arrest was intercepted by the secretary to the president for scrutiny. He obviously felt a need to know those who sympathized with the former government employees who were under house arrest.

When I learned of this development, God led me in a decision. Writing a letter to the president would be the proper way for a missionary to address the matter. My three-page letter included an event that would shed light on our attitude toward the Korean leader. It was to be the turning point in our remaining in Korea.

Shortly after taking office, President Chun Doo-hwan took members of his cabinet on an official visit to Burma, now Myanmar. Korean media reporters and other national leaders made the trip. The goodwill visit was to encourage trade between the countries.

On the Sunday morning of his trip, an event occurred in the church that I included in the letter to the president. As the morning sermon was beginning, I told the worshipers that there was a need for special prayer. I asked them to join me in a prayer for the Korean president, who was in a foreign country. It was the work of the Holy Spirit; I had not planned it.

The intercessory prayer occurred at the exact time of the following event. In Burma, there is a Martyrs' Mausoleum in Yangon, the city that held an official parade of welcome on that Sunday morning for the Korean president. The Korean ambassador to Burma led the parade in his car and was followed by the presidents of the two countries in their official vehicles.

The tremendous crowd at the parade moved into the path of the vehicles causing them to stop. The ambassador's vehicle was able to slowly proceed while those following waited for the crowd to be moved. Being free of the crowd, the ambassador proceeded to the mausoleum.

Upon his arrival, two North Korean agents waiting in an abandoned service station remotely detonated a bomb in the mausoleum that killed twenty-one and injured forty-six. Seventeen South Koreans including the ambassador and five cabinet members died in the explosion.

The North Korean agents had exploded the bomb prematurely because they had heard the presidential bugle announcing what they thought was the arrival of the Korean president. The ambassador's arrival, mistakenly taken for that of the president, had prompted the blast.

In the weeks following the detectives' questioning of me, the president received my letter that mentioned my unplanned prayer for him. I received a call from his secretary. He said the President wanted me to meet with him, but I did not know why. The secretary asked me to come with two or more missionaries, and we arranged a time.

On the day of the meeting, two career missionaries attended the meeting with me. At the appointed time, the secretary arrived. He said that the president had been called suddenly, on an emergency, to the demilitarized zone, a free area between the two countries.

The secretary insisted on having the meeting. The President had told him what he wanted to discuss. The secretary assured us he would relay our concerns to the President.

President Jimmy Carter had visited South Korea. In a widely publicized magazine article, he had criticized its leaders for a few things he had observed. As a devout Christian, he was deeply concerned about religious freedom and mentioned that in his article. That was the subject of our meeting. President Chun wanted to know how Korea could provide complete freedom of worship and religion. The meeting lasted two hours or more. The older missionaries were explicit in outlining their beliefs and experiences. The secretary was polite and asked serious and meaningful questions.

Because South Korea was primarily a Buddhist country, Christians making fast inroads in the country sometimes faced opposition. There had been a Billy Graham crusade and other large Christian gatherings there without hindrance, but there were reports from the rural areas that local officials were hindering Christians from doing their work.

As of this writing, religious freedom is a reality in South Korea. The hospital and theological school founded by Baptist missionaries are staffed by Korean Christians. There are no missionaries of the Southern Baptist Convention serving in South Korea today. The goal of converting and training nationals by dedicated missionaries in Christian life and service has made this possible. South Korea is now a country that sends out Christian missionaries.

It would be arrogant for me to think our meeting could have changed the ancient religious practices of a people. It was an opportunity only God could provide for the freedom of His people. The results were in the plan of God for the expansion of His kingdom. God's personal plan for each of those created in His image included every soul in Korea.

CONCLUSION

> I have kept the faith. Now there is in store for me the crown of righteousness, which the Lord, the righteous Judge, will award to me on that day. (2 Timothy 4:7–8)

T he apostle Paul was certain of his faith in the Lord Jesus Christ. He had an attitude all Christians should admire. Faith can never be a wish; it must be a certainty based on a never-wavering expression of trust in God each moment of life. It involves daily repentance, renewal, communication through prayer, waiting, and serving a God of love.

Oswald Chambers, who died in 1917 while working in an Egyptian camp ministering to soldiers, seemed to have one major theme. His argument for service in the Lord was based on a single fact. His goal was to have every move of his life reflect evidence of God's nature in him. (*My Utmost for His Highest*, page 239).

John, the "beloved disciple," made clear how God guided sinners. Jesus said the His Spirit, would take up residence in His disciples (John 14:20).

There has been a challenge in traveling over the world. The tendency is to get angry when seeing how leaders enslave their people especially in Russia and China. There is a strong urge for anger to replace prayer. The difficulty is yielding when God leads. Oswald Chambers said this means to go when He says, "Go!" to forgive when He says, "Forgive!" and to stop when He says, "Stop!" These are vital thoughts for one who has the nature of God in him by the presence of the Holy Spirit.

The influence of the Evil One, Satan, opposes the leading of God. Be assured that his influence never leaves humans and especially dedicated believers. The world is his domain, which requires purposeful yielding to the Spirit's leading. The more we yield to the strong power of the Lord's leading, the greater the power we have to ignore Satan's influence.

The most difficult thing to overcome is the love of evil in society. This is universal. There is no place to hide. Therefore, the desire to please a loving God comes with the need for continuous renewal, a continuous prayer of forgiveness, and a continuous seeking the quiet but sure leading of the Holy Spirit.

Our journey has been one of joy in the Lord! God's plan is glorious. His providence for believers is always one step ahead of Satan and the world. His will is to see us in glory with Him eternally. When we yield to Him, God appoints timely and wonderful angels to see that our journey is complete. It is to His glory. Praise Him!

Printed in the United States
By Bookmasters